The King's Gambit Bible is here

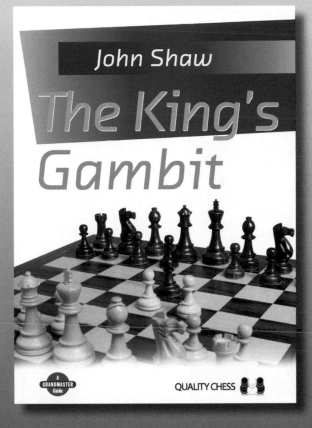
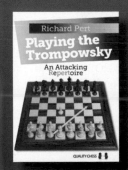

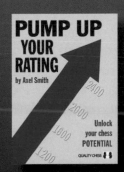
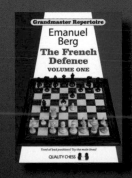
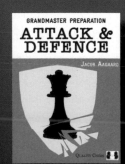

2013 Issue 7
NEW IN CHESS

PUBLISHER: **Allard Hoogland** EDITORS-IN-CHIEF: **Dirk Jan ten Geuzendam, Jan Timman**

12 Vishy Anand
38 Interview
24 St.Louis
52 World Cup

'At one of the tournaments in Gausdal, in the summer of 2000, my wife was watching Magnus play and she said, it looks like he is suffering. I want to take him under my arm and bring him home. And she asked him after the game: was it painful? And he looked at her astonished, he didn't understand at all. And I explained to her that chess players are extending themselves, they are putting an effort in this.' – Henrik Carlsen

SUBSCRIPTIONS p.128

COLOPHON

PUBLISHER: Allard Hoogland
EDITORS-IN-CHIEF:
Dirk Jan ten Geuzendam, Jan Timman
CONTRIBUTING EDITOR: Anish Giri
EDITORS: Peter Boel, René Olthof
ART-DIRECTION: Jan Scholtus
PRODUCTION: Joop de Groot
TRANSLATORS:
Sarah Hurst, Ken Neat, Piet Verhagen
SALES AND ADVERTISING: Remmelt Otten

© No part of this magazine may be reproduced,
stored in a retrieval system or transmitted in any
form or by any means, recording or otherwise,
without the prior permission of the publisher.

NEW IN CHESS
P.O. BOX 1093
1810 KB ALKMAAR
THE NETHERLANDS

PHONE: 00-31-(0)72-51 27 137
FAX: 00-31-(0)72-51 58 234
E-MAIL:
SUBSCRIPTIONS: nic@newinchess.com
EDITORS: editors@newinchess.com
SALES AND ADVERTISING:
otten@newinchess.com

BANK DETAILS:
IBAN: NL41ABNA 0589126024
BIC: ABNANL2A in favour of Interchess BV,
Alkmaar, The Netherlands

WWW.NEWINCHESS.COM

CONTRIBUTORS TO THIS ISSUE
Yochanan Afek, Simen Agdestein, Dmitry Andreikin, Jeroen Bosch, Pavel Eljanov,
Anish Giri, Jon Ludvig Hammer, Vladimir Kramnik, Alexander Motylev, Hikaru
Nakamura, Peter Heine Nielsen, Lennart Ootes, Hans Ree, Jonathan Rowson,
Matthew Sadler, Sergey Shipov, Nigel Short, Jan Timman, Evgeny Tomashevsky,
Maxime Vachier-Lagrave, Wei Yi, Hou Yifan
PHOTOS AND ILLUSTRATIONS
Alina l'Ami, Phil Bath, Anastasiya Karlovich, Dagobert Kohlmeier, Alexander
Motylev, Rosa de las Nieves
COVER PHOTO
Magnus Carlsen: New In Chess

Ten months to go

If need be he was going to run himself, he had stated at various occasions, so that is what he is going to do. In Tallinn, during the 84th FIDE Congress, Garry Kasparov announced his candidacy for the FIDE presidency. At a festive reception in the ballroom of the Swissôtel, the 13th World Champion launched his campaign in front of FIDE delegates, journalists and other assorted guests, by presenting his ticket. A ticket which 'represents every continent and a mix of business and investment expertise, organizational backgrounds, and chess experience'.

Three of its members were present and addressed the meeting: Afrika Msimang, a social activist and teacher, who is the president of the Kasparov Chess Foundation South Africa; Belgian businessman and entrepreneur Jan Callewaert, who is the president of the Kasparov Chess Foundation Europe; and Ignatius Leong, arbiter and organizer from Singapore, who is currently FIDE General Secretary. Video messages were shown of the other two team members: Sheikh Mohammed bin Ahmed Al Hamed of the United Arab Emirates, a businessman with a military background who owns various five-star hotels, including the spectacular Jumeirah Beach Hotel in Dubai; and Rex Sinquefield of St. Louis, an investor whose Dimension Fund Advisors oversees more than $300 billion and whose Chess Club and Scholastic Center needs no introduction for the readers of this magazine (and if so, have a look at page 24 ff.).

A remarkable member is Ignatius Leong, who holds a prominent position in FIDE today, but who also has a record of friending and unfriending, or at least trying to, current FIDE president Kirsan Ilyumzhinov. Apparently, Leong has come to the conclusion that it's high time that the international image of chess becomes respectable again. Chess seems to be thriving with more and more activity at all levels,

but in the public eye its reputation is at a low level. Typical was a preview of the match in Chennai in *The Economist* with observations that make the true chess fan cringe. Such as 'Yet despite booming interest in the amateur game, top-level chess has become obscure again, hobbled by squabbles and eccentric leadership'. Or 'Its boss since

Garry Kasparov and his wife Dasha at the launch of the Kasparov 2014 campaign in Tallinn.

1995 has been Kirsan Ilyumzhinov, who also ran Kalmykia, one of Russia's poorest regions, until 2010. That year Mr Ilyumzhinov said he was contacted by aliens; in 2011 he played chess with Muammar Qaddafi.'

Naturally, Kasparov promises to change all this and to make FIDE a transparent organization dedicated to the interests of both amateur players and professionals. On the campaign website Kasparov2014.com, he lists '6 winning moves'. Practically all of them voice ambitions that can hardly be argued with, from improving FIDE's finances with corporate sponsorship, via the promotion of chess as an educational tool, to changes in the rules that will make the game more attractive and fight any form of cheating. Some sound ambitious, but raise questions about how they can be accomplished, such as 'a universal rating system (that) will include every game of chess played on the planet, from world championship matches to online blitz. It will serve as a portal that unites tens

of millions of players and will become an attractive advertising and sponsorship asset.'

The elections will be held on August 14th, 2014, at the Chess Olympiad in Tromsø. Till that day Garry Kasparov will be travelling around the globe to promote his views and to explain in further detail how he intends to restructure and strengthen FIDE. And to prove that his boasts will not be empty ones. Such as the promise of Ilyumzhinov's ticket before the previous elections that Afrika Msimang reminded the guests in Tallinn of in her speech. That four years ago FIDE promised to invest 400,000 euros annually for the development of chess in Africa. Money that the chess players in Africa are still waiting for.

And who will be Kasparov's opponent in the elections? At the Congress in Tallinn, Kirsan Ilyumzhinov held a long speech summing up his achievements and avoiding the subject of the elections with jocular remarks that campaigns are a waste of money and that this money is much better invested in school chess. Only when, at the end of his speech, he was urged to reveal whether he was running or not, did he state that he was.

Ilyumzhinov's behaviour seemed to suggest nervousness, but that may be only outward appearance. Through the years he and his team have gained huge experience in handling elections. One of the big challenges for the Kasparov team will be how to deal with their opponents' expertise at exploiting the one-country-one-vote rule.

Those were the days

Tournament books have become a rarity these days. Perhaps we may even conclude that they will soon be an extinct species. Therefore it is laudable that there are publishers who re-issue classical tournament books, if only to remind us how much pleasure such works can bring. And it is even better if a classic becomes available in English for the first time. A Dutch classic that will now reach a broader audience is the book that Max Euwe wrote on the World Championship tournament in 1948 in The Hague and Moscow, where Mikhail Botvinnik ascended the throne that had been

Hanon Russell and Fietie Euwe with the 'first copy' of The Hague-Moscow 1948.

vacant after Alexander Alekhine's death in 1946. The book launch of *The Hague-Moscow 1948* became a historical moment in itself. At the Max Euwe Centre in Amsterdam, American publisher Hanon Russell presented the first copy of the book to Fietie Euwe, the youngest daughter of the fifth World Champion, who was barely two years old when her father won the highest chess title by beating Alekhine in 1935.

Those shoes are made for...

It was a short-lived and controversial career, but few will regret that it's over. Borislav Ivanov, the Bulgarian chess player under unanimous suspicion of large-scale cheating (see New In Chess 2013/5, p.6), has announced the end of his 'chess career'. On the Bulgarian website Blitz.bg, Ivanov declared that the psychological front against him is too strong and that he can no longer stand all the accusations and insinuations. He had wanted to be a GM, but apparently that is not going to happen. The last straw was a search at a tournament in Blagoevgrad that he was subjected to

at the express wish of one of his opponents, GM Maxim Dlugy. Not trusting Ivanov after having seen some of his games, Dlugy insisted on the search and asked to be there, together with a friend of his, to give instructions. The security officer went along with this request as long as he could search Dlugy in the same manner. A proposal that Dlugy happily accepted. He felt he was on to something and the events proved him right. His hunch was that Ivanov had a computer hidden in his shoes that he worked with his toes. And so at the end of the search came the request: 'And now take off your shoes', with the example set by Dlugy who took off his own shoes and socks. This was where Ivanov's cooperation ended. He categorically refused to take off his shoes, claiming his socks smelled. They could forfeit him, but no way was he going to take off his shoes. Funnily, he wasn't forfeited and appeared for the next game, but if there was any remaining doubt it had been dispelled by his decisive reaction. Various observers now also mentioned the funny way Ivanov walked, as if his shoes didn't fit properly. Dlugy drew his conclusions and apparently so did Ivanov. Good riddance.

Now that he has cut this knot he may also do us a further favour and explain how exactly he did it. And why.

Borislav Ivanov: Time enough now to think when he will tell us how and why.

Cash and Garry

During the second game of the final of the World Cup in Tromsø, Garry Kasparov joined the live broadcast via Skype. For more than an hour he shared his views and answered questions from the hosts and the viewers. One spectator asked which actor Kasparov would prefer to play him if a movie was to be made about his life. Apparently, this was a

Joaquin 'Garry Kasparov' Phoenix?

question that others (or he himself) had asked (himself) before, as he replied without any hesitation: 'Joaquin Phoenix.' A good choice, we may say. It would be fascinating to see how the American, who rose to fame with his role in *Gladiator* and his portrayal of Johnny Cash in *Walk the Line*, would 'interpret' Garry Kasparov.

Maybe one day he will. Disney recently announced that they have acquired the screen rights to Matt Charman's 'The Machine', the high-tech dramatic re-telling of the 1997 Man vs. Machine chess match between Garry Kasparov and the IBM super-computer Deep Blue (see New In Chess 2013/5, p.6). Charman will adapt his play, which premiered in Manchester and had a month-long run at the Armory Theatre in New York City. Once the script is ready, they can start racking their brains who to ask for the lead role. ∎

Perfect opponent

I have never written elucidative letters or defended myself in any such way, but having read Mr. Chess Conflict Number One's comments on our game from the Grand Prix in Beijing (New In Chess 2013/6, pp. 93-95) and the interesting afterword he wrote, I understood that the time has come.

1. 'My opponent walked around watching the remaining games for about 10 minutes...'

I wonder, was Topalov recording the time?! How come 5 minutes became 10? It's no secret that during most classical games I rest 3-7 minutes before returning to the board to give myself a break after the first time control. Not a single opponent or referee has ever complained about that. I am sorry that Veselin happened to be the only one offended.

2. 'Nor did he show up at the press conference after the game...'

An extremely interesting claim, as my final press conference after the last round can be easily found online.

The point of such accusations is simple and clear – blackening me to provoke top tournament organizers not to invite a player of such 'bad behaviour'.

A bit illogical in this story is that Veselin has beaten me in three Grand Prix tournaments, winning all our encounters in a very easy, instructive and one-sided way. Largely thanks to those wins he won the entire series. Why make so much noise, and make far-fetched claims, against such a perfect opponent?

Alexander Morozevich
Moscow, Russia

Revolutionaries

While Adam Feinstein and I may disagree, perhaps, on a few issues, I did enjoy his cover story in New In Chess 2013/6, as it took me back to my childhood. Never since reading in March 1953 an obituary of Comrade Joseph Stalin was I presented with such a loving description of a great and good human being, nor did I see so many loving notes of revolution.

I understand that we chess players like to read about the rich (Pagel, Van Oosterom, Kok, Sinquefield), the famous (Einstein) and the powerful (Napoleon, Nicholas II, Krylenko, Che, Vaclav Klaus), who play(ed) chess and patronize it, and are willing to view

them overall favourably because of it. Still, one can cover Krylenko, as Sosonko did, without the syrupy sweet Feinstein used on Che: '(T)he women can't take their eyes off him', '(D)espite his charm and openness Guevara had an austere streak' …

So did, I guess, such charmers and 'revolutionaries with a passion for chess' as Krylenko and Goebbels (*Genosse* Goebbels chaired the German Chess Federation).

Lev Alburt
New York, USA

A Stalinist communist

New In Chess is famous worldwide for its high quality journalism and, over the years and decades, has become one of the best chess journals in the world. It is rightly a prestigious publication.

But, in your last issue, New In Chess 2013/6, you have published 'Che and Chess', an unbelievable article which mainly praises a so-called 'revolutionary' who was nothing less than a Stalinist communist.

Did Mr. Adam Feinstein want to write a 'vulgate' or a hagiography? Did he, at least, read *The Black Book of Communism* (French original edition 'Le Livre Noir du Communisme', 1997), in which the reality and not the myth of Che Guevara is presented (Part 5, Chapter 1)?

As an example: Che Guevara was Public Prosecutor and created the first

Cuban gulag, or 'forced labour camp' or 'work corrective camp' in 1960. Soviet Stalinist society was his ideal society.

Other sources are most probably available for confirmation.

But, by the way, who is Mr. A. Feinstein? His credentials are not even presented.

And how is it possible that nobody at New In Chess read the article before publication and said 'No! It cannot be published'? So why did you decide in favour of such a superficial publication? How could you accept such an article? I think it is indeed damaging and detrimental to New In Chess. The editor should consider to apologize to the readers.

As for myself, I will send you back my copy, for I don't want to keep this issue at home.

Philippe Briffaut
Loreto, Italy

Editorial postscript:
Adam Feinstein is currently working on a book about cultural policy in Cuba since the Revolution. His biography, *Pablo Neruda: A Passion for Life*, was published by Bloomsbury in the UK and the USA in 2004. His latest book, *A History of Autism: Conversations with the Pioneers*, was published by Wiley-Blackwell in the UK and the USA in 2010.

A psychopath

I was extremely dissatisfied today when I received the 2013/6 issue of New In Chess. Portraying a cold-blooded murderer on the front page of the best chess magazine was very, very bad taste.

I do not care if he liked to play chess or went, with his expenses paid by the enslaved people of Cuba, of course, to watch important tournaments or befriended great masters like Najdorf.

The fact is that he was a psychopath who enjoyed killing people. Recently, a lot of books have demystified the image and myth that was created around him, especially through the famous picture of Alberto Korda.

I thought that only in Third World countries he was still a hero, but it must be remembered that even Fidel sent him away to the jungle of Bolivia, where he was killed with the help of the same people he wanted to 'help'.

I bet that in prisons all over the world there are people who enjoy playing chess. Why not put them on the cover?

David Borensztajn
Rio de Janeiro, Brazil

Emoticons (1)

In New In Chess 5/2013, Steve Giddins complained about the use (or rather abuse, in his eyes) of 'little squiggles', which he thinks is totally despicable in chess commentary.

Although he particularly refers to GM Anish Giri, I know that many other GM's use this way of expressing themselves in their notes, which, I think, they have adopted from the way people chat these days.

His point was that the vast majority of the readers of this magazine are native English speakers, who don't need such ways of expression, because they can very well understand what is being said or intended without them.

Maybe this is right, but nevertheless, for a minority among the readers (such as myself), English is not their mother tongue. Yes, we understand and read English, but these expressive emoticons help us to understand what is written in a funny way.

I think that New In Chess is an international chess magazine edited in English, with lots of readers from multiple nations who make an effort to read in English. So, I am grateful to Anish Giri and all other GM's that use emoticons for their help to improve our understanding!

Antonio Maset
Santa Fe, Argentina

Emoticons (2)

As a keen New In Chess reader I would like to congratulate you on a fine publication. I enjoy the insights from the top players. Nigel Short's articles are always entertaining.

But the greatest thing about your publication is the use of emoticons, as the dry and humourless nature of many chess books makes them a difficult read. I always enjoy writers who inject humour into what is a very difficult subject. Chris Ward, Simon Webb and Bruce Pandolfini come to mind.

So, it is refreshing when reading to see a little smiley face. It is a nice juxtaposition between a very serious art form and a light-hearted form of expression.

Could you perhaps one day publish an issue consisting entirely of emoticons rather than words? This would make me feel ☺

Dave Cork
Crawley, Sussex, United Kingdom

Missing moves

In Jan Timman's article 'The same excellent fish' in New In Chess 2013/6, on the game Negi-Cheparinov from the Politiken Cup in Copenhagen, he says:

Negi-Cheparinov
position after 23...dxe5

'After 24.d6 ♖c6 25.♕e4! ♕c5 26.♗c4! and Black is powerless...'

What does Jan Timman have in mind after the obvious 26...♕xc4? I could not see a win for White after that... I tried Houdini which said 27.d7 ♕xe4 28. dxe8♕ ♕xc2+ 29.♔a1 ♖c8 30.♕d7 e4 31.♕xb7 e3 etc. White sacrifices his queen, then queens a pawn and wins Black's rook. White finally wins Black's e-pawn, but has to trade queens and loses back his c-pawn.

Then you wind up with Black down the exchange, but he has an extra pawn and draws. White would win if he could trade rooks, but Black can avoid that. It is a fascinating position.

Actually, in the original position Houdini suggested not 23.d5 but 23. ♗d3 for White.

Steve Brudno
Brookline, MA, USA

Postscript Jan Timman:

There were two moves missing. In my analysis of White's 24th move in Negi-Cheparinov, the variation should read as follows: 24.d6 ♖c6 25.♕e4 ♕c5 and now first 25.d7 ♖d8 and only then 26.♗c4. Now on 26...♕xc4, 27.♕xe5 ♗g7 28.♕e8+ wins.

Such a beautiful gesture

Hans Ree's article 'In a blaze of light' in New In Chess 2013/5 brought back two memories of Mikhail Tal at the New York Open, 1990. When his game with Kamsky ended with a win for Gata, Tal stood up and shook Kamsky's hand. This took place on a stage where the top four boards were set. A very big deal at the time when other players from the Soviet Union were avoiding Kamsky big time.

Before the first games of one day and while strolling through the central hall with two other men, two boys (twelve or so) and with one carrying a camera, noticed Tal. One of the boys approached Tal and communicated that he would enjoy having his photo taken with him, and when Tal smiled the boy handed his camera to his friend. Tal shook his head and took the camera from the boy, passing it to one of his friends, placed himself between the two boys with an arm around each boy's shoulder, and had the photo taken. Such a beautiful gesture, one that I feel fortunate having witnessed.

Please thank GM Ree for his work for your magazine over the years.

Peter Hardman
Rhinebeck, New York

Jacqueline Piatigorsky

Patron, Player, Pioneer

J

Just like the fine arts, chess has always been largely dependent on the passion and vision of wealthy patrons. Jacqueline Piatigorsky (née de Rothschild), who died last year at the respectable age of 100, was an ardent chess player herself, but will primarily be remembered for the tournaments that she organized together with her husband Gregor Piatigorsky, the renowned cellist.

The Piatigorsky Cups, held in 1963 and 1966 in Los Angeles and Santa Monica, gathered the world's best players and set a new standard for elite events. The exhibition *Jacqueline Piatigorsky, Patron, Player, Pioneer* is on view from October 25, 2013 to April 18, 2014 at the World Chess Hall of Fame in St. Louis. Among the exhibits is this fine photograph from the 1966 tournament of Jacqueline Piatigorsky modestly watching Bobby Fischer and Boris Spassky, the ultimate winner, after their draw in Round 17(!). Clearly the American and the Russian were already on excellent terms well ahead of the World Championship match in 1972 that would forge a lifelong friendship.

A Person of Indian Origin

In 2000 Vishy Anand, age 31, became World Champion for the first time, by winning the FIDE knock-out World Championship tournament in New Delhi and Tehran.

Jonathan Rowson

I was born in Aberdeen to white Scottish parents and hold a British passport, so it was quite a surprise when, in my early thirties, I managed to become 'A Person of Indian Origin'.

I have the documentation stamped by the Indian consulate in London to prove it, and my marriage to Siva, who holds an Indian passport, to thank for it. The 'origin' reference is a bureaucratic relic, and the document is a glorified visa pretending to be a passport, but in a manner of speaking I am Indian now.

Except I'm not, and probably never will be. Although I have been to India several times in the last decade, she remains fundamentally foreign to me,

as she will be for most people watching the World Championship match in November. Which makes me wonder: How much does it matter, to Anand, to Carlsen, to all of us, that the match will take place in the World Champion's home town, in the country that gave birth to the game?

Move by move, it won't matter much at all. Unlike most sports, there is no roar of the crowd, no flags fluttering in the wind, no particular sense of home advantage. However, while the *result* of the match will be decided over the board, India has a direct bearing on the *meaning* of the match, which matters to the watching world, but also has a subtle impact on the players' psyches, who might try to think only of their next move, but cannot help but be characters in an unfolding global drama.

Although chess originated in India, before Anand there were few signs

of national ownership. The game was recognised as a sport, but until the nineties it was merely a renegade activity for the small minority who refused to conform to the ritualised worship of cricket. Anand's international achievements made the game not merely popular, but also respectable and admirable, and there is now a huge market for the teaching of chess, particularly in Delhi and Chennai which are the main chess population centres. I heard a great story that the profitability of chess coaching led one yoga teacher to manually change the paint on his advertisement board from 'XYZ Yoga Academy' to 'XYZ Chess Academy' and thereby profit by a 500% rise in income.

Some believe Vishy being World Champion is a crucial part of this growth in interest, and fear this era of pride and expansion may be coming to an end, but this prognosis misses

Indian journalists follow Vishy Anand around the world, but there are always many more when he plays in his home country, such as at his Candidates' match against Gata Kamsky in Sanghi Nagar in 1994.

a big part of Vishy's charm. It's not just that he is a world-beating player, but more simply that his character is inviting. He invariably looks smart, happy, friendly and self-possessed; the kind of person your average middle-class family in India would be happy to feed at home with Idli and Sambhar. It is important to understand this mix of charms that informs Vishy's popularity because they have created a singular kind of progress. As Susan Polgar put it: 'The impact that Vishy made for chess in India is unsurpassed. He is a national hero in his homeland and he revolutionized Indian chess.'

While it is clear that Anand made chess in India, it is less clear that the reverse applies. My reading of Vishy's unwritten biography is that he is a man who is genuinely grateful for his roots, but never allowed himself to be tethered by them. On the one

'Vishy has always been sattvic. His energy is latent and pure, he is free of intoxicants, thinks lucidly, and speaks clearly and well.'

hand he is part of that Indian establishment, and for instance was the first sports person to be awarded the second highest civilian honour, the Padma Vibhushan, in 2007, an honour shared with other global icons like

Ravi Shankar and Sachin Tendulkar. On the other hand, he rarely leads an Indian chess team and keeps his distance from most Olympiads.

In light of such tensions, Vishy has skilfully managed his reputation in a country where the media loves to provoke controversy. I have spent many hours watching Indian news channels and it is striking how they manufacture drama out of dust; a careless word here or there by a sports star can dominate the news cycle. Vishy however manages Indian press interviews with considerable skill. His answers feel honest and satisfying rather than evasive, but they are never scurrilous or speculative. He steers clear of misinformation and gossip.

While there has been no media scandal, there has been some fun relating to his endorsements. My inlaws in Bangalore tell me that over

CHESSBASE 12

NEW!

Start your personal success story now. ChessBase 12 is the chess database program which has become the world-wide standard. Get to know your next opponent'sweak points and exploit the advantage of targeted preparation. Enjoy the new ChessBase 12 program with fantastic new analysis and search features!

New in ChessBase 12:

"Deep analysis" generates a dynamic tree of variations. Leave the analysis running as long as you want. The longer the running time, the more reliable the variations displayed. Variations which do not hold up at the greater depth of calculation are automatically excluded. The result is commentary containing analysis of the important candidate moves. Strong improvement over the deep position analysis in Fritz, because it can run forever, all the while adapting the variation tree with ever-increasing depth.

Team up engines from different systems in a **"Cloud analysis".** This is a deep analysis done by several engines working in parallel, which saves an enormous amount of time. The engines are running on other computers, where they can be set up with a few clicks. You can even make the engines undertake different tasks: one engine always directs the analysis. Another spends all its time calculating the candidate moves in the starting position, in order to obtain the optimal depth of calculation. Then there is one or more other engines which are looking for the replies to each of the candidate moves etc.

"Similarity search": In ChessBase 12 endings can now be looked for with a single click and displayed classified according to their similar-

ity to the position on the board. Access to a whole heap of endings with the same distribution of material on modern 64-Bit systems is gained in a few seconds only. And what works with endgames can also be transferred to middlegame positions. In this case too, a search is instigated for pawn structures which are almost similar to the position on the board and the similarity is considered on the basis of the position of the pieces.

More improvements:

• Online player encyclopedia with Elo ratings, upgraded throughout the year

• "Let'Check": access the world's largest database of in-depth analysis (more than 5 million positions)*

• Optional 64Bit version: speeds up access to your databases

• Intelligent google-style search box for the ChessBase online database with now more than 6,4 million games*

• New look for the ChessMedia window, big database symbols for high resolution

• New engine dialog with CPU-optimisation

• One-click publication of one or more games on the web in a Java script.

System requirements: Minimum: Minimum: Pentium III 1 GHz, 1 GB RAM, Windows Vista, XP (Service Pack 3), DirectX9 graphics card with 256 MB RAM, DVD-ROM drive, Windows Media Player 9 and Internet access to activate the program, Playchess.com, Let's Check, Engine Cloud and updates.

Recommended: PC Intel Core i7, 2.8 GHz, 4 GB RAM, Windows 7 (64 Bit) or Windows 8 (64 Bit), DirectX10 graphics card (or compatible) with 512 MB RAM or more, 100% DirectX10 compatible sound card, Windows Media Player 11, DVD ROM drive and Internet access to activate the program, Playchess.com, Let's Check, Engine Cloud and updates.

 ChessBase 12 - Starter package 179,90 €

• ChessBase 12 Program
• Big Database 2013
• Games download until 31st December 2013
• Access to ChessBase Online Database (over 6.4 million games)*
• Access to "Let's Check" and "Engine Cloud"
• Half a Year's subscription to ChessBase Magazine (3 issues)

 ChessBase 12 - Mega package 269,90 €

• ChessBase 12 Program
• Mega Database 2013
• Games download until 31st December 2013
• Access to ChessBase Online Database (over 6.4 million games)*
• Access to "Let's Check" and "Engine Cloud"
• Year's subscription to ChessBase Magazine (6 issues)

 ChessBase 12 - Premium package   369,90 €

• ChessBase 12 Program
• Premium membership on playchess.com (1 year)
• Mega Database 2013
• Games download until 31st December 2013
• Access to ChessBase Online Database (over 6.4 million games)*
• Access to "Let's Check" and "Engine Cloud"
• Year's subscription to ChessBase Magazine
• Corr Database 2013 + Endgame Turbo 3 (9 DVDs)

 ChessBase 12 - Upgrade from 11   99,90 €

• ChessBase 12 program
• Access to ChessBase Online Database (over 6.4 million games)*
Only after you have returned your CB11 registration number!

*) the service lasts till 31.12.2015

CHESSBASE GMBH · OSTERBEKSTRASSE 90A · D-22083 HAMBURG · TEL ++(49) 40/639060-12 · FAX ++(49) 40/6301282 · WWW.CHESSBASE.COM · INFO@CHESSBASE.COM
CHESSBASE DEALER: NEW IN CHESS · P.O. Box 1093 · NL-1810 KB Alkmaar · phone (+31)72 5127137 · fax (+31)72 5158234 · WWW.NEWINCHESS.COM

the years Vishy has appeared in quite a few different kinds of commercials. Most recently he was advertising a product that is basically paracetamol, and Saghamitra Chakraborthy from Grey PR who promoted this brand described why they needed Vishy as follows:

'Well, this product is for cold and flu. What we're trying to say is that it not only clears the symptoms but it *actually clears your mind*, and *that's the reason* why we chose Viswanathan Anand.'

So now you know. If you want to clear your mind, get a cold and take a pill endorsed by the world chess champion. Having watched a few of these adverts, I think it's fair to say that for all his talents Vishy is not God's gift to acting. Whenever he looks into the camera and smiles, his eyes seem to be saying, above all, when are you going to stop filming?

Vishy also makes a big charitable impact. In the national newspaper, *The Hindu*, last year I came across the following story, expressed in quintessentially Indian English:

'Ever since five-time world chess champion Viswanathan Anand got back from Moscow after his triumph over Boris Gelfand in the 2012 championship, he has been grandly felicitated for this achievement. There was one more felicitation function on Saturday, but this one, like nothing he had ever experienced before... Dr Agarwal's Eye Hospital felicitated Anand by committing to perform 100 free cataract surgeries for poor patients... every year.'

Such a gesture goes beyond any 'grand felicitation' and surely left Anand in no doubt that his work over the chessboard has a very direct impact on the lives of people less fortunate than himself. Of course it's great to be responsible for a chess explosion, helping to bring a lifetime of absorption and joy to thousands. However, there are 18 million blind people in India, 55% of them due to cataracts, and now a 100 peo-

ple a year will be given their sight back directly because of Vishy's success.

On hearing such stories, it is easy to describe Vishy as 'nice' or 'impressive' or any other garden variety adjective, but to understand Vishy's secret, you need to grasp that he is, above all, sattvic. There is no quick way to explain what that means, so it is worth a short digression. In Vedantic Philosophy, the relative world features three qualities of life, 'gunas', that correspond to manifestations of energy. Sattva is potential energy, manifest in balance, stability and purity; rajas is energy in motion, restless, unstable, changing, enervating, and tamas is burnt out or otherwise static energy, lethargic, dull, slow, inert or deluded. We need a little bit of everything, but spiritual seekers are advised to be as sattvic as possible. Kasparov had a great deal of rajas, Fischer latterly succumbed to ramas, but Vishy has always been sattvic. His energy is latent and pure, he is

free of intoxicants, thinks lucidly, and speaks clearly and well.

But now this natural propensity to sattva will be tested. In the context of the current challenge, I find it hard to imagine how Vishy's psyche could remain stable and focussed and not collapse into overactivity or dark imaginings. How can he find the will to prepare to compete in a world championship match for the *fourth* time in less than a decade?

And of course now the challenge goes deeper than that, because it's Carlsen. Vishy is faced with the prospect of a young and versatile hunter coming down from the Northern Hemisphere to invade his homeland, and slay and dethrone him in front of his people. That imaginative framing may sound dramatic with respect to kings and queens and pawns, but at the level of India, myth and meaning, it's exactly what Vishy has to contend with. ∎

DAGOBERT KOHLMEIER

For special events and ceremonies Vishy Anand and his wife Aruna sometimes like to dress up and choose from their Indian wardrobe.

'For all his talents Vishy is not God's gift to acting.'

Anand–Carlsen The Stats

Who's the favourite in the eagerly awaited World Championship match in Chennai? Current World Champion Vishy Anand holds a positive score against Magnus Carlsen and no active chess player has more match experience than the Indian. On the other hand, the Norwegian has been the undisputed number one in the world rankings for 27 consecutive months and has won the most recent encounter with the Champion. The rating difference of a whopping 95 points suggests a sweeping 7-4 victory for Carlsen, but how much weight do their ratings really carry? **Lennart Ootes** collected further statistics that may play a role and may improve your insight before you place your bets!

Youngest World Champions
Garry Kasparov (22)
Anatoly Karpov (24)
Mikhail Tal (24)
Emanuel Lasker (26)

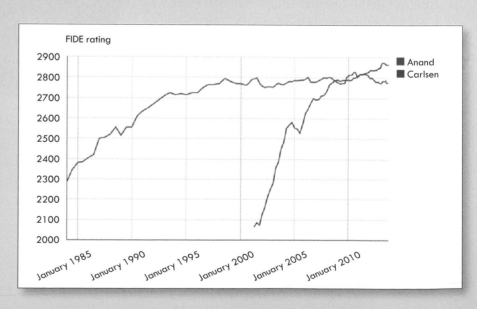

Viswanathan Anand	Passport name	Magnus Øen Carlsen
December 11, 1969	Birth date	November 30, 1990
Madras (Chennai), India	Birth place	Tønsberg, Norway
Chennai, India	Place of residence	Oslo, Norway
2775	Current rating	2870
7	World ranking	1
At age 6 from mother	Learned chess	At age 5 from father
1985 / Age 15	International Master	2003 / Age 12
28-12-1987 18 years, 17 days	Grandmaster	26-04-2004 13 years, 4 months, 26 days
2004, 37 years old	#1 on rating (for the first time)	2010, 19 years old
1997, 1998, 2003, 2004, 2007, 2008	Chess Oscar	2009, 2010, 2011, 2012
Karpov (19 out of 34, +4) Kasparov (18 out of 48, −12) Kramnik (40 out of 77, +3) Smyslov (½ out of 1, =0) Spassky (1½ out of 2, +1) Tal (1 out of 1, +1) Topalov (30½ out of 59, +2)	Score against World Champions	Anand (13 out of 29, −3) Kramnik (10 out of 20, =0) Topalov (10½ out of 16, +5)
+18 = 12 −5. Lost to: Marta Litinskaya (1988) Alisa Maric (1988) Judit Polgar (1991, 1988, 1999)	Score against women in classical chess	+15 = 13 −5. Lost to: Tatjana Plachkinova (2001) Olita Rause (2002) Gabriela Hitzgerova (2002) Elena Sedina (2003) Kateryna Lahno (2004)
7	Number of Olympiads	4
Kasparov (-12) Aronian (-4) Nakamura (-3)	Negative score against	Volokitin (-4) Anand (-3) Nepomniachtchi (-3)
Shirov (+13) Adams (+12) Piket (+9) Timman (+9) Leko (+8) Khalfman (+8) Van Wely (+8) J.Polgar (+7) ... Karpov (+4) Kamsky (+4)	Excellent score against	Radjabov (+7) Nakamura (+7) Adams (+6) Topalov (+5) Dominguez (+5)

Age difference in World Championship matches

1894: Steinitz-Lasker (32)

1960: Botvinnik-Tal (25)

2013: Anand-Carlsen (21)

1921: Lasker-Capablanca (20)

World Championship matches without Russians/Soviets

Steinitz-Zukertort (1886)

Steinitz-Gunsberg (1891)

Steinitz-Lasker (1894)

Lasker-Marshall (1907)

Lasker-Tarrasch (1908)

Lasker-Schlechter (1910)

Lasker-Janowski (1910)

Lasker-Capablanca (1921)

Anand-Carlsen (2013)

Carlsen's World Championship record

2004: FIDE knock-out Tripoli, lost 1st round to Aronian

2005: World Cup Khanty-Mansiysk, lost 4th round to Bareev

2007: Candidates' matches Elista, lost 1st match to Aronian

2007: World Cup Khanty-Mansiysk, lost semi-finals to Kamsky

2013: Candidates' tournament London: winner

Anand's major tournament victories

World Junior Championship (1987)

Asian Championships (1989)

Wijk aan Zee (1989, 1998, 2003, 2004, 2006)

Reggio Emilia (1991)

Dortmund (1996, 2004)

Linares (1998, 2007, 2008)

Dos Hermanas (1997)

Melody Amber (1994, 1997, 2003, 2005, 2006)

Leon (1999, 2000, 2001, 2005, 2006, 2007, 2011)

Corsica (2001, 2002, 2003, 2004, 2011)

Baden-Baden (2013)

Total tournament and match victories: 104

Top year: 1998 (Wijk aan Zee, Linares, Madrid, Frankfurt, Tilburg)

Top-10 youngest GMs 1988

Bobby Fischer	1958	15
Garry Kasparov	1980	17
Boris Spassky	1955	18
Simen Agdestein	1985	18
Viswanathan Anand	1987	18
Anatoly Karpov	1970	19
Nigel Short	1984	19
Julio Granda	1986	19
Ivan Sokolov	1987	19
Vassily Ivanchuk	1988	19

Anand vs Carlsen

Rapid/Blitz: 33 games - Classical: 29 games

	Anand won	Carlsen won	Draw
Rapid/Blitz	9	8	16
Anand White	5	4	8
Carlsen White	4	4	8
Classical	6	3	20
Anand White	2	0	11
Carlsen White	4	3	9

Top-10 youngest GMs April 2004

Sergey Karjakin	2002	12
Magnus Carlsen	2004	13
Bu Xiangzhi	1999	13
Teimour Radjabov	2001	14
Ruslan Ponomariov	1997	14
Etienne Bacrot	1997	14
Peter Leko	1994	14
Andrei Volokitin	2001	15
Koneru Humpy	2002	15
Hikaru Nakamura	2003	15

Classical encounters by year

	2007	2008	2009	2010	2011	2012	2013
Anand	½ 1 1 ½	1 1 ½ ½ ½	0 ½ ½	½ 1 ½ ½ ½ 1	½ ½ ½ ½ ½	½ 0 ½	½ ½ 0
Carlsen	½ 0 0 ½	0 0 ½ ½ ½	1 ½ ½	½ 0 ½ ½ ½ 0	½ ½ ½ ½ ½	½ 1 ½	½ ½ 1

Anand's World Championship record

1990: FIDE: Qualifies for Candidates' matches at Manila Interzonal

1991: FIDE: Candidates' matches, loses in quarter finals to Karpov

1993: PCA: Qualifies for Candidates' matches at Groningen Interzonal

1993: FIDE: Qualifies for Candidates' matches at Biel Interzonal

1994: FIDE Candidates' matches: loses in quarter finals to Kamsky

1994-1995: PCA Candidates' tournament: beats Kamsky in final

1995: PCA World Championship match: loses to Kasparov

1997: FIDE knock-out tournament Groningen: beats Adams in final

1998: FIDE World Championship final: loses to Karpov

2000: FIDE knock-out World Championships: beats Shirov in final

2002: FIDE knock-out World Championships: loses to Ivanchuk in semi-finals

2005: FIDE World Championship tournament San Luis: 2nd after Topalov

2007: World Championship tournament Mexico City: winner

2008: World Championship match Bonn: beats Kramnik

2010: World Championship match Sofia: beats Topalov

2012: World Championship match Moscow: beats Gelfand

Score in classical games in 2013

Carlsen: 34 out of 51, +21, =26, -4, TPR 2877

Anand: 31 out of 56, +14, = 34, -8, TPR 2798

Months

	Anand	Carlsen
Months #1	21	39
Months Top 5	237	63
Months GM	303	114

Carlsen's major tournament victories

Wijk aan Zee (2010, 2013)

Tal Memorial (2011, 2012)

Melody Amber (2010)

London (2009, 2010, 2012)

Bilbao (2011, 2012)

St Louis (2013)

Biel (2007, 2011, 2012)

Nanjing (2009, 2010)

Bazna (2010, 2011)

Total tournament victories: 32

Top year: 2010 (Wijk aan Zee, Nice, Bazna, Arctic Stars, Nanjing, London)

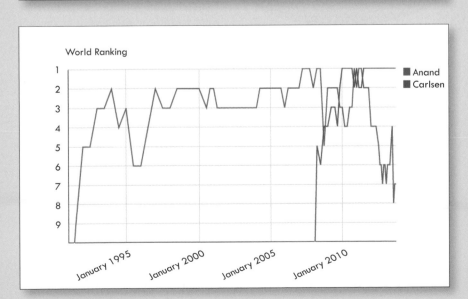

World Ranking

■ Anand
■ Carlsen

H

Sergey Shipov

How to beat Magnus Carlsen

How to beat Magnus Carlsen? This is currently the most topical question. Such a domination of one player over the rest has not been seen now for 15 years, since the previous millennium. And it is even more difficult to remember when this was done by a player who was not the World Champion.

Naturally, many want to dispute the power of the 'dominator'. But I do not see any point in considering abstractly the question of defeating him, since a very simple prescription suggests itself – play more strongly and more quickly than Magnus. You have to operate at the strength of the best programs on a powerful computer, and success will be guaranteed. But such advice applied to a human is fruitless. Usable resources have to be found. For a specific person – and we know his name from the posters of the forthcoming match.

Chess is a game for two, a system of two communicating vessels. And therefore the question 'How to beat Carlsen?' should be expanded to 'How can Anand beat Carlsen?'

I will begin with some historic analogies.

Imagine that you were asked early in 1927: 'How to beat Capablanca?'

How is it possible to defeat a player who has won all the tournaments in succession and over a period of seven years has lost only two games? How to find spots on the sun? And the reply suggests itself – there is no way! Well, apart from placing Capablanca in a heavenly place where there are many beautiful women…

At the time there were few who bet on Alekhine, so strong was the belief in the World Champion's infallibility. Up till then he had not lost to the challenger in their individual meetings; he had an advantage in points and in the character of the play. But – you will remember how the match concluded. Capablanca turned out to be a living person, and his chess and competitive weaknesses were exposed. Incidentally, in Buenos Aires women were indeed involved. But I do not think that this was part of the preparation by the Russian champion…

A question of roughly similar complexity faces me now.

Carlsen has already been the strongest player in the world for five years, and his victories have become as regular as the change from day to night. In contrast to Capablanca, he works a lot on chess and for the moment he successfully parries attacks by the fairer sex.

Magnus's strength lies in his total universalism. He plays well in any positions and almost any openings, and he is a fighter to the marrow of his bones, flexible, stable and cool-headed.

In style and in his approach to chess, Carlsen is an improved version of Spassky, strengthened by the latest achievements of chess theory. In independent play in the top tournaments the Norwegian plays at practically the strength of the best programs. For example, from the statistics in London 2013, more than anyone else his moves coincided with the computer's first line.

How then can he be defeated?

The search for a new Fischer suggests itself. A chess maniac at the height of his powers is needed! But Anand is no such player. And he also does not resemble Alekhine. Not the same character.

I have studied all the Norwegian's defeats over the past few years and have discovered their mechanism.

V. Anand	M. Carlsen
🇮🇳	2817	🇳🇴	2823

More precisely, its complete absence! Magnus himself is the instigator of his failures. Few have succeeded in completely outplaying him. Mainly the Norwegian himself has overstepped the mark.

It can be confidently said that some of Carlsen's mistakes leading to bad results are impossible in a World Championship match. For example, the clear under-estimation of the opponent, excessively creative play, obvious and deliberate ignoring the demands of the position, and so on. After all, the Norwegian realizes that on this occasion the price of defeat will be too great.

However, here it is a question of measure. After all, Magnus is **accustomed** to playing for a win in almost all playable positions, he is constantly aiming for a fight, and he always and everywhere feels that he is stronger than the opponent. Will he be able to curb his habit and subordinate it to the demands of a match for the title?

The last time Vishy Anand defeated Magnus Carlsen was in a rapid game at the Botvinnik Memorial in Moscow in 2011.
His last classical win goes back to the 2010 London Classic.

Not necessarily! In the heat of the battle and if he is rather tired, he will not necessarily be able to control himself 100%. So that here Anand has a chance. His task is to catch Carlsen at that moment when he overestimates his position. And at the right time readjust from playing for a draw to aggression. This is difficult, but possible.

In the opening stage Carlsen does not shine. Just like Spassky, he constantly avoids fashionable lines, provoking his opponent into independent play as soon as possible. Direct computer analyses in topical varia-

tions have never been Magnus's forte. But Anand has many times demonstrated such an ultra-deep delving into opening positions. Remember his wins against Kramnik in the Meran Variation in Bonn in 2008! Hence he must work out the probable openings and delve seriously into them – to set traps for Magnus.

In positions that are distant from opening preparation, in general and on the whole, Carlsen is stronger than anyone on earth. But this is only in general and on the whole. In 'his' positions every strong grandmaster can perfectly well fight against a monster. And if Vishy is able to lure his opponent into structures for which he has a subtle feeling (and there are many of them), there he may be able to pose problems for the challenger. The phrase 'able to lure' again returns us to opening preparation. There much will be decided.

But, as is known, it is not enough to gain an advantage and even outplay

Carlsen. To win a game, you have to overcome stubborn resistance, figure out inevitable complications and (or) withstand the tension in the conversion stage. For this you need technique and physical endurance. You have to maintain your concentration all the time at a high level – this is difficult. Difficult? Very! But not impossible.

There is another recommendation for the Champion that suggests itself. It suggests itself, but it is not unquestioned.

If you remember how Anand defeated Carlsen in previous years (Carlsen-Anand, Wijk aan Zee 2008, Carlsen-Anand, Morelia/Linares 2008, Carlsen-Anand, Bilbao 2010, Anand-Carlsen, London 2010), they were, as a rule, very sharp battles. By no means slow positional manoeuvres, but sacrifices, mutual attacks and unclear complications. Thus it is in this type of fight that Anand's pluses show up most clearly on the background of Carlsen's minuses. This is obvious, but… But everything moves, everything changes. And it's almost three years ago that he won that last game.

Can Vishy now demonstrate his earlier intensity and accuracy of calculation? In the end, at a mature age even Tal began changing his style, and he regularly scored wins by performing the role of a dry, cautious player.

Initially Kasparov did not regard the young Carlsen as a strong tactician. He thought that he did not play well in dynamic positions. Of course, by his own high standards. But Magnus's positional play impressed Garry. The young player's pieces always moved to the right squares.

In principle, even today there is a strong grain of truth in such arguments. Carlsen sometimes feels uncomfortable in unstable and quickly changing positions. And there is a temptation to lure him into such play.

But!... The problem is that to find an opponent who would feel confident in such situations is almost impossible. For this you need the young Tal, Shirov or Kasparov himself. And not the ageing Anand.

It may happen that, by luring Magnus into positions that are unpleasant for him, Vishy will make things even more unpleasant for himself. And he himself will fall into the trap that he has set for his opponent.

And if it is taken into account that Anand is an ageing player, that to change and readjust to circumstances will be increasingly difficult for him… It turns out that the World Champion should think above all about himself. Do things so that he feels comfortable, and what his young opponent is thinking about and how he is feeling should be a secondary matter….

As you see, I myself have arrived at a definite conclusion. But here I will try to argue further. Yes, in playing for complications there is a risk. But perhaps the risk is justified? After all, if everything else is even worse, perhaps the **least evil** should be chosen?

Carlsen has another small flaw – his vision of the board geometry. Sometimes he completely overlooks nonstandard piece manoeuvres. Do you remember how he did not see the move 30.♗h8! in the last round of the Candidates' Tournament against Svidler? This is symptomatic. However, there are also other examples.

Carlsen-Svidler
London Candidates' 2013
position after 29...♗b7

Here Carlsen continued 30.♗h4, which combined with his next move 31.f3 (after 30…♕c6) landed him in a lost position. Instead, he could have played 30.♗h8! which gives White a clear advantage after 30…♕c6 31.f3 ♖e7 32.♖f1 ♕d6 33.♔g2 (see New In Chess 2013/3 for Peter Svidler's extensive notes to this dramatic game).

Therefore Carlsen's opponent should regularly study seemingly strange manoeuvres, unusual piece placings – they may well come as an unpleasant surprise for the Norwegian.

It is also noticeable that Carlsen regularly goes wrong in rook endings. But can you show me a person who plays them ideally? Rook endings are objectively the most difficult to play. They are highly concrete and full of the most subtle nuances. So that Carlsen's mistakes, which have become famous, are fully excusable, and no one, including Anand, is ensured against them. Vishy himself has several times lost drawn rook endings.

Moreover, the well-known principle 'Against young players, aim for the endgame!' is categorically unsuitable for battles with Carlsen. He is markedly stronger than all his rivals, including Anand, in endings in particular – especially in complicated, practical endings, where there is dynamic play and there are numerous fundamentally different lines. Partly this is associated with the fact that Magnus simply has more endurance

'Carlsen's opponent should regularly study seemingly strange manoeuvres, unusual piece placings.'

than his opponents, and that he keeps his standard of play very high in the fifth and even the sixth hour of play. Therefore it will be extremely difficult for Anand to keep up with the young bull in drawn-out games. He won't have the strength.

Thus it turns out that the path to victory for the World Champion is very narrow and unsteady. After weighing up everything for and against, I will endeavour to suggest some brief chess recommendations:

1 He must forcefully, with a computer-like grip, take Carlsen 'by the throat' in the opening. Obtain positions studied at home, in which the key variations and plans are known.

2 It would seem that sharp positions with the queens on will give Vishy the best chances. And he should not put off the crisis until later. The earlier a stern battle begins, the easier it will be for the veteran.

3 Anand should study many candidate moves, not excluding seemingly strange manoeuvres. In so doing, of course, with an eye on the clock, since severe time-trouble is inadmissible.

And now, about the main thing!

Much in a battle between equal or nearly equal opponents is decided by psychology. You must constantly believe in yourself, and, if possible, put pressure on your opponent. Karpov and Kasparov demonstrated models of such pressure. With their every step, gesture and glance they put pressure on the opponent, breaking his will to resist.

What are they thinking? In 2008 38-year-old Vishy Anand beat 17-year-old Magnus Carlsen 4-2 in a rapid match in Mainz.

In this respect Anand's possibilities are restricted – he is not able to press, and he does not possess the character of a killer. On the other hand, he is capable of holding on and maintaining his composure under pressure. The collapse in his first World Championship match with Kasparov became a stern and valuable lesson for him. Subsequently in the battle for the title Vishy has demonstrated the stability of his nervous system.

Now he may be oppressed by Carlsen's general superiority as a chess player. And with this he has to fight! The match should begin with a clean slate, 'forgetting' all the results of the past five years. The mood should be such that sitting opposite will be a strong and well-studied player, but without a history of victories. Then the sub-conscious barrier (how can you beat someone who himself constantly wins everything?) will be lifted. This was precisely Alekhine's problem. He was able to 'forget' about Capablanca's victories and play the match without deference towards his opponent. And Anand is quite capable of doing this.

The World Champion should also adopt the example of another of his great predecessors. Even when he was older and was objectively inferior to young opponents, Karpov always retained the **psychology of a winner**. He was able (and, probably, is able even now), when not playing at his best, to make 100 moves in a difficult battle, at the same time believe in his lucky star, and seek a possibility of seizing the initiative – thanks to which a mistake by the opponent on the 101st move is immediately exploited. The result is a seemingly illogical win, but it is logical precisely from the standpoint of Karpov's approach to the battle. If Anand can play like this in the match, he will be able to exploit his chances, of which there are unlikely to be many.

Thus, the most important recommendation:

4 Vishy must believe in victory. In any position, in any competitive situation. He must not crack or lose heart. However difficult things are. Only in this case will there be a chance. So that possibly the World Champion's best assistant will be a yogi. A spiritual mentor. A sensei. ∎

With four players the Sinquefield Cup was relatively small in size. But it felt like a festival. The Saint Louis Chess Club, the World Chess Hall of Fame, and Lester's, a popular sports café next to the club, were barely big enough to receive everyone that wanted to witness the first-ever Super GM tournament in the American capital of chess. Magnus Carlsen was supposed to be the star of the inaugural Sinquefield Cup, and the star he was. While all players had to pose for countless photos and sign autographs, the excitement went in overdrive whenever Carlsen mingled amongst the fans. The Norwegian also delivered on the chessboard, winning the $70,000 first prize with an imposing 75 per cent score. In the process he raised his rating to a telling 2870 on the eve of the World Championship match against Vishy Anand.

NEW IN CHESS

Dirk Jan ten Geuzendam

First Sinquefield Cup is for Carlsen

I

'If you had told me five years ago what it would be, I would have had you locked up in the loony bin.' We're having a coffee at Starbuck's, one of the businesses on Maryland Avenue that have profited from the chess invasion in this upscale part of St. Louis. From the corner of his eye, Rex Sinquefield watches the crowd on the other side of the street, engaged in a game of chess or just enjoying the glorious autumn weather outside the St. Louis Chess Club. Next to our table two kids are dragging around the big pieces of the outdoor chess set on the doorstep of the World Chess Hall of Fame. They are big pieces, but still they look minuscule compared to the giant king in front of the museum that claims to be the biggest chess piece in the world. Sinquefield looks genuinely amazed as he continues: 'It has so far exceeded my expectations. Everybody else's. Basically what happens is that every time we try something, it seems to work. But that's because we have very good staff. First of all I am surprised how fast things go. They are going better than we could have ever expected. If you had told me five years that we'd be in over a hundred schools, I would have thought you were crazy. But we are in over a hundred schools. It's done

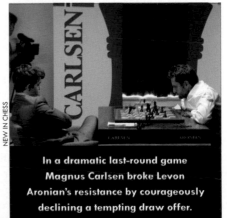

In a dramatic last-round game Magnus Carlsen broke Levon Aronian's resistance by courageously declining a tempting draw offer.

by the club. We hire people, they go into the schools. I think we have about 20 full and part-time workers, it's a lot.' And the club blossoms as well. 'We have the largest membership for clubs in the United States, and we have never advertised for members. I couldn't believe how fast we had hundreds of members in the first year or two. From all over the area. We've had a good number of people moving to St. Louis because of the club. That's unbelievable.'

With a grin he adds: 'My wife has a funny line, she said: "My husband said he was going to start a chess club

With live commentary, an endless supply of food and drink and more than enough television screens, Lester's, the sports café next to the Chess Club, was a perfect place to follow the games.

and I thought, how expensive can that be?"' He laughs. She will know by now. He agrees: 'It's more expensive than I had thought, but what I will say, worth it. It's worth doing for the city and for chess.'

First there were the US Championships that revived a tradition going back to 1886, when Steinitz and Zukertort played four games of the first World Championship match in St. Louis. Next there were small, expertly run events with an international flavour, such as friendly matches between Nakamura and Ponomariov or Seirawan and Karpov. And then the World Chess Hall of Fame found a new home in a splendidly renovated house across the street of the club. 'The Hall of Fame dropped in our lap. The U.S. Chess Trust called me, can you take it over? People in Miami can't do it. I said, sure. But it's become much more than it ever was, and much more than we'd expected. Combining art, both the visual arts and the musical arts that are related to chess, into this venue. Four times a year we change exhibitions. They don't need to be pure chess, but they ought to be related to chess.'

The next logical step was an international tournament, an idea that was in the pipeline for a couple of years. The wish was a top event including the number one player in the world rankings, Magnus Carlsen. In the end, the inaugural Sinquefield Cup had four players: the two top-rated American GMs versus the two highest rated players in the world. As ambitions can never be suppressed in St. Louis, the second Sinquefield Cup has already been announced for next year, this time with six players. Needless to say that the ultimate ambition is to have a World Championship match in St. Louis, an ambition Rex Sinquefield is not secretive about. 'That I'd definitely like to do. But circumstances have to be right. I've said publicly that I'd love to do that sometime.'

Rex Sinquefield: 'My wife has a funny line, she said: "My husband said he was going to start a chess club and I thought, how expensive can that be?"'

The name of the tournament does not reflect the vanity of the sponsors. The idea to call it the Sinquefield Cup came from advisers around Rex and Jeanne Sinquefield and was inspired by the legendary Piatigorsky Cups in 1963 and 1966. An apt inspiration, as the Piatigorskys and the Sinquefields have a lot in common in their support for chess. It was particularly well-timed that the tournament coincided with a preview of an exhibition about the Piatigorsky Cup in the Hall of Fame (see pp.10-11). Both couples set standards of excellence with their tournaments, continuously trying to raise the prestige of the game and looking for innovations that show their commitment. For instance, Jacqueline Piatigorsky experimented with demonstration boards on which the moves were projected instead of being executed manually by board boys and she commissioned two tournament books, now classics, with the games annotated by the participants. For the Sinquefield Cup, exquisite Staunton pieces were commissioned to replace the 'ordinary' DGT pieces. Frank Camaratta of House of Staunton had to solve a few technical issues to have the pieces weighted without interfering with the transmission signals, but he managed and the result was simply beautiful.

Perhaps the biggest difference between the Sinquefields and the Piatigorskys is the extent of the involvement of both partners. While Gregor Piatigorsky was mainly happy to morally support his wife's passion, Jeanne Sinquefield's role cannot be overestimated. Apart from being directly involved in countless activities at the club, her biggest achievement so far has been the introduction of the Chess Merit Badge for the Boy Scouts of America. It's a huge success and already 40,000(!) boy scouts have earned the badge. With the same boy scouts in mind, she had a portable chess set designed. Extremely portable, we can say, as the small pouch with flat pieces on a small stick and a paper board, weighs virtually nothing and fits easily in more things than a small rucksack.

With their previous tournaments the Sinquefields had already shown their fine eye for detail and their fortunate hand when picking staff. With their first international event the St. Louis Chess Club even surpassed their earlier efforts. The Internet spectators could follow the action with live commentary by Jennifer Shahade, Yasser Seirawan and Maurice Ashley, superbly filmed by an extensive television crew. The fans who came to St. Louis were even better off. For $15 a day (and the rate only got better if you stayed longer) you could follow the games at the club, in the Hall of Fame or in Lester's restaurant, a sports bar next to the club. Here, additional commentary was provided by Varuzhan Akobian, Ben Finegold, Ronen Har-Zvi and Ian Rogers, and everywhere there was free food and drink. With a mixture of pride and surprise, Rex Sinquefield told me that earlier in the day he had run into a neurosurgeon who had taken a week off from work and driven here from Mississippi. 'Check that on the map. That's a long drive!'.

Magnus Carlsen was supposed to be the star of the event, and the star he was. While all players had to pose for countless photos and sign autographs, the excitement went in overdrive whenever Carlsen emerged from the playing room. The Norwegian played the starring role with consummate ease, taking his time at press conferences and obliging his fans. Said Sinquefield: 'He is very personable. I

was told he was very nice, and that's indeed what he is.'

And Carlsen delivered on the chessboard, winning the $70,000 first prize with an imposing 75 per cent score, 4½ out of 6, a full point ahead of Nakamura, two points ahead of Aronian and no fewer than three points ahead of Kamsky. The winner called his score 'flattering', but here, too, the old dictum may ring true that you get what you deserve. Perhaps we didn't see Magnus Carlsen at his very best in St. Louis, and his personal analysis of his performance will be a critical one, but he fought in all his games, didn't drown when the waves looked threatening and used his chances when his opponents wavered. The most impressive moment he saved till the last round, when he showed the grit that he hopes will play a crucial role in the upcoming match in India. Having survived an unpleasant middlegame, he didn't embrace Aronian's draw offer and the tournament victory that came with it, but did what the situation asked him to do. He saw chances in the position

and felt that his opponent was on the verge of breaking. His choice was the right one. Aronian didn't have a second wind and collapsed under the pressure.

Carlsen triumphed as a fighter who wanted to win, but wasn't obsessed by a wish to play streamlined and flawless games. Typical was his comment when he was asked if he'd been hiding opening preparation and whether his choice of the Dutch Defence was part of that: 'I think the Dutch Defence was more the result of being in a particularly good mood. I think in this tournament most of the games were decided over the board, in the middlegame, in complicated fights, rather than in preparation.'

The only player who came close to challenging Carlsen was Nakamura. The American Number 1 won his first two games and was leading halfway the event after a draw in Round 3 against Carlsen. During both this game and that in Round 5 against the top-seed, Nakamura wore sunglasses. On the day of the first encounter with his bête

As the grandmasters played their games inside, the tables outside the Chess Club were permanently occupied by a steady stream of visitors eager to fight their own battles.

noir, he had been talking to a friend on Skype who had said, why not wear sunglasses? And so he went to the mall and bought a pair. 'I just wanted to do something different. What's the worst that can happen? I lost enough games against him already and I can't really do much worse than losing.' Actually it felt great and he didn't have to think long what to do in the second game. 'Well, it worked the first time, so why not? There's no rhyme or reason as to why. It was not that I wanted to throw him off.'

Was Carlsen thrown off by the sunglasses? It didn't seem so and when he was asked what he thought of his opponent's decision, he did the wisest thing he could do: he shrugged his shoulders and said nothing.

Given the way Nakamura started, he was obviously a bit disappointed by the final outcome, although he remained realistic. 'If you'd asked me before the tournament if I'd be happy with plus one, then I certainly would have said

yes. Obviously, in retrospect, I am not so happy with it. It's all relative. I could have very easily drawn against Levon (Aronian) yesterday, but I had no business winning the first game. All the luck I got in this tournament evened out for me. But just having that opportunity and letting it slip is a bit disappointing.'

Indeed, his win in the first round against Aronian could safely be called a lucky break.

Nakamura-Aronian
position after 30...♘xc5

There isn't much going on, and after 30...♕c6 the game would no doubt have ended in a draw. **30...♕b5?** A grave oversight, or a temporary lack of concentration, costs Aronian dearly. **31.♕xb5 axb5 32.♘d7**

Black loses the exchange and the game, as the resulting position is an easy win for White. **32...♖xd7 33. ♖xd7 ♖a8 34.♔f2 ♖a6 35.g4 ♘h4 36.f4 ♖c6 37.♖e8+ ♔g7 38.♖ee7 ♖f6 39.♔g3 g5 40.f5 h5 41.♖e6** Black resigned.

Hikaru Nakamura played both games against Magnus Carlsen wearing sunglasses. 'What's the worst that can happen? I lost enough games against him already and I can't really do much worse than losing.'

In hindsight one can say that Aronian never really recovered from this unfortunate loss. He had his revenge in the second game, when Nakamura missed the best defence, but the Armenian failed to show the deep and many-sided chess he is rightly famous for. The psychological blow that he suffered in the last round against Carlsen was a horrible way to end a tournament that was never his.

Gata Kamsky had to settle for last place. The American champion took a decision that was greatly appreciated. Instead of playing his usual rock-solid chess, hoping for an acceptable score in this elite company, he chose to have some fun and opted for more adventurous play. In the end he didn't get what he deserved, but didn't complain. 'I love this place, the atmosphere, the club and the people, the way they organize things. This was a great chance to show the American chess fans the chess we can play. In a tournament like this we don't have to worry about the result, but can play exciting chess, make the fans go, wow, he played this move! If I want to play solid, the way I usually do, I can do that, but that's not interesting.'

Kamsky still plans to quit chess when he is 40, but till that time he intends to play as much as possible. And he might continue after 40 if Fischerandom becomes more popular. 'I have the feeling that in five, ten years from now, people will find that Fischerandom is the best chess. Right now we have this scientific approach, everyone is spending way too much time analysing the openings. Fischerandom will be a return to normal chess. No more analysis, no more scientific approach, you just come to play chess. And in the time you save you can do other things in life. You can get degrees, get an education. I always liked chess, it always gave me pleasure, but I always hated studying. Chess should be just that game that we play. I would like to see chess as a sport and an art, not as a science.'

Kamsky was Carlsen's most generous opponent, losing both games. The first one was a fine achievement by Carlsen, which you will find annotated by his second Jon Ludvig Hammer. In the second game he played with an uncharacteristic lack of determination. Having outplayed Kamsky from the black side of an Exchange Ruy Lopez, he missed several moves and needed some further mistakes from his opponent to haul in the full point after all. After the game Carlsen was in a bad mood and quickly left for his hotel. It was generally assumed that he was annoyed by his sloppy play in the endgame, but there was more to it, as he only revealed at the prize-giving. During the fourth hour he had been increasingly upset by a rock group playing outside that disturbed his concentration. So when he was asked if he was happy with the tournament he said that he was very happy with everything apart from these moments at the end of his game against Gata. For next time, he suggested with a grin, they should have a banner asking for no music within a mile of the club. Everyone laughed, but I wouldn't be surprised if in their permanent wish to improve they will really take measures to prevent this from happening again.

> On the day of the first encounter with his bête noir, Nakamura had been talking to a friend on Skype who had said, why not wear sunglasses?

NOTES BY
Jon Ludvig Hammer

SL 3.1 – D15
Magnus Carlsen
Gata Kamsky
St Louis 2013 (1)

1.♘f3 ♘f6 2.c4 c6 3.d4 d5 4.♘c3 a6 5.e3 ♗f5 6.♗d3

White swaps bishops, leaving Black with a 'good' one, but in return White gets quick development and is ready to go e4, opening up for his remaining bishop. **6...♗xd3 7.♕xd3 e6 8.0-0 ♗b4 9.♗d2**

9...♗xc3 Even the worst bishop is better than a knight, a saying goes. By putting the bishop on b4 Kamsky made it clear that he was prepared to give it up in the hope that White's bishop would be restricted by its own pawns. The surprising thing is that he exchanged it without being probed by a3.

By doing so he avoided potential tactics like 9...0-0 10.♘xd5 ♘xd5 11.cxd5 ♗xd2 12.dxe6, sacrificing a piece, although Black should be very much okay here.

10.♗xc3 0-0 11.a4 ♘bd7 12.a5 ♘e4 13.♗b4 ♖e8 14.♖ac1

14...h5 Yes, it's a strange move – there's no denying that. But strange doesn't necessarily mean bad. As the game progressed, gaining space on the kingside actually made lots of sense! **15.♘e5 ♕c7 16.♘xd7 ♕xd7**

17.♕e2 With this move, I think Magnus started drifting. Kamsky gets to retreat his knight from a vulnerable square in the centre without f3/e4 coming with tempo. With White's bishop controlling the dark squares, he needs to take control of the light squares. Something like 17.f3 ♘f6 18.e4 ♖ac8 19.♗c3 looks tremendously comfortable for White. **17...♘f6 18.♖fd1 ♕c7 19.h3 ♖ad8**

20.b3
Black is well coordinated in the centre. Any attempt to go f3-e4 will be met by an immediate counter: 20.f3 e5.
20...♖d7 21.♕c2 ♕d8 22.♖cc1
The very definition of drifting has to be: going aimlessly back and forth. After the game Magnus jokingly quipped that this was an excellent strategy, as Kamsky became very optimistic about his position, going all out for a win!

22...h4 23.♗e1 ♘e4 24.♕g4 g5
Black gets going with a strong initiative on the kingside. If I were playing White, I'd certainly be nervous, but Magnus keeps his cool.
25.cxd5 f5 26.♕f3 cxd5 27.♖c2 ♖g7 28.♖dc1 ♘f6
28...g4 feels more to the point, but White keeps the upper hand after 29.♕f4 gxh3 30.f3.
29.♕d1 g4 30.f3

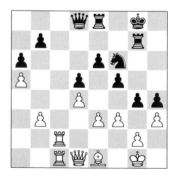

Suddenly the rook on c2 comes into its own: a defender on the second rank, and an attacker on the c-file.
30...gxh3 31.♗xh4 The attacker has become the attacked. The bishop is opening a second front on the kingside together with the queen, while

the rooks are looking intimidating on the c-file. Black is already much worse.

31...♔f7

31...hxg2 32.♕e1 ♕e7 33.♖c7 ♔f8 34.♖xg7+ ♕xg7 35.♕g3 doesn't seem all that dangerous for Black, but if we follow the computer's first line, we see that White's strong bishop, with some help from its king, will create huge problems:

ANALYSIS DIAGRAM

35...♕xg3 36.♗xg3 ♖e7 37.♔xg2 ♖d7 38.♗e5 ♘h7 39.♔g3 ♘f8 40.♔h4 ♘g6+ 41.♔g5 ♘xe5 42.dxe5 ♔g7 43.♖c8.

32.♕e1 hxg2 33.♖c7+ ♖e7 34. ♗xf6 ♔xf6 35.♖c8 ♕d6 36.♕h4+ ♔f7 37.♕h5+ ♖g6

As his friend and second Jon Ludvig Hammer watched the livestream, Magnus Carlsen 'found all the accurate moves and got his king walking through the minefield to find safety on f3.'

Watching the live stream, I felt confident there was a mate somewhere, but it's not so easy to find. Magnus found all the accurate moves and got his king walking through the minefield to find safety on f3.

38.f4 ♕a3 39.♕h8 ♖g7 40.♕h5+ ♖g6 41.♕h8

After this very professional repetition of moves I was sure Magnus would win. By repeating he made the time-control, and now he could take his time to find the correct moves.

41...♖g7 42.♕f8+ ♔g6

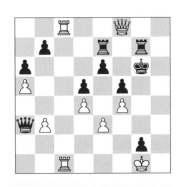

43.♔xg2

This is the absolutely only move to win in this position. Black can give a discovered check with his king, but

once the white king gets to f3, it will be safe.

43...♖gf7

44.♕d8

It's important to make sure that the black rook stays on f7, as witness the following variation: 44.♕g8+ ♖g7 45.♕d8 ♕b2+ 46.♖8c2 ♕xb3 47.♔f3 ♔f7 48.♖c8 ♖g3+ 49.♔xg3 ♕xe3+, and Black suddenly gets his counterattack going just in time.

44...♖h7

44...♕b2+ 45.♖8c2 ♕xb3 46.♔f3 wins with a check on the g-file next.

45.♖g1 ♕a2+ 46.♔f3+ ♔f6 47.♕g8 ♖h3+ 48.♖g3 ♖xg3+ 49.♕xg3

Kamsky resigned, as 49...♖g7 50.♖f8+ ♖f7 51.♕g5 mate settles the issue.

NOTES BY
Hikaru Nakamura

SI 41.9 – B43
Hikaru Nakamura
Gata Kamsky
St.Louis 2013 (2)

In short events it is often critical to get off to a good start, as momentum is far more important. With two consecutive Whites to start the tournament, it was imperative that I tried to do something. Fortunately for me, things could not have gotten off to a better start, as I would win both my first round against Levon Aronian and the following game against the 2013 U.S. Champion, Gata Kamsky.

Much has been made about a potential rivalry between myself and Gata, but I have never really felt this. While we are both fierce competitors, we have nothing but respect for each other. Furthermore, whenever the team events roll around, we are always there to help out the other one.

1.e4 c5
Throughout the tournament, it seemed that Gata's goal was to experiment and try to play exciting games. While the results were a bit unfortunate, I think the fans greatly enjoyed the fighting spirit. Therefore, it did not really surprise me that he chose 1...c5 over 1...e5.
2.♘f3 e6 3.d4 cxd4 4.♘xd4 a6 5.♘c3 b5 6.♗d3 ♗b7 7.0-0 ♘c6 8.♘xc6 ♗xc6 9.♖e1 ♕b8

10.a4
An improvement over a previous

game I had in this exact same line, except from the black side.
After 10.♕e2 ♗d6 11.e5 ♗c7 a draw was agreed in the game Gashimov-Nakamura from Wijk aan Zee 2012.
10...b4 11.♘d5 ♗d6 12.♕h5

12...♘e7
A new try. Another try was 12...♗xd5, but this hardly solves anything: 13.exd5 ♘f6 14.♕g5 ♔f8 15.dxe6 dxe6 16.♕h4 and once again, Black is substantially worse due to the bad king position. This was played in Tiviakov-Perez Candelario, Malaga 2003.
13.♘xe7 ♗xe7 14.b3!?
The computers give White an advantage after 14.e5 g6 15.♕g4 h5 16.♕d4 ♕b7 17.f3, but I don't particularly understand why. I feel that Black should be solid enough.

14...a5!?
A rather strange move, and one which was played instantly. While ...a5 is logical it doesn't seem absolutely necessary or critical in this moment.
During the game I saw 14...g6 15.♕h6 ♗f8 16.♕h4 ♗e7 17.♗g5 ♗xg5 18.♕xg5 0-0 and figured it was equal or slightly better for me.
However, I do think that with correct

play Black should have no problems.
15.♗b2 ♗f6

16.♗xf6
Another interesting move was 16.e5!?, but I felt that after 16...♗e7 17.♗d4 ♕b7 18.♕h3 ♖c8 I should have a small advantage but nothing tangible. That is why I opted for a more direct and straightforward approach.
16...gxf6 17.e5 ♖g8
After 17...f5 18.♖ad1 ♕b6 19.♗c4 White stands significantly better.
18.g3 ♖g5

19.♕h6!
19.♕xh7 ♖xe5 is absolutely nothing for White and Black can start to fight for the initiative.
19...♖xe5 20.♕xf6 ♖h5 21.♗e4 ♕d8 22.♕f3 ♖c5

23.♕e3?! While I saw the variation 23.♗xc6 ♖xc6 24.♖e4! ♖ac8 25. ♖g4 ♔e7, I stopped my calculations here as I thought I could easily end up worse. However, I underestimated the attacking ideas: 26.♖d1 ♕c7 (26...♖xc2 27.♖g7 ♕f8 28.♖xf7+ ♕xf7 29.♖xd7+ ♔xd7 30.♕xf7+ ♔d6 31.♕f4+ ♔d5 32.♕f3+ ♔e5 33.♕e3+ ♔d5 34.♕d3+ ♔e5 35.♕xh7, and White should be winning here with accurate play) 27.♖f4 ♖f8 28.♖fd4 d5 29.♖e1 ♔d8 30.♕f6+ ♔c8 31.♖f4, after which White is better, but it is very hard for a human to calculate these lines.

23...♕e7!?

A very practical and human decision which complicates matters.

Strangely enough, I thought I was better in the ending after 23... ♖e5 24.♕d4 ♖xe4 25.♖xe4 ♗xe4 26.♕xe4 h6 27.♖d1, as I would win the h6-pawn for the c2-pawn, but the computer seems to hold this quite easily for Black: 27...♖c8 28.♕h7 ♖c3 29.♕xh6 ♖xc2 30.h4 ♕b6 31.♕f4 ♕c5, and if anything, White has to be careful to maintain the balance.

24.♗xh7 f5 25.♗g6+ ♔d8 26. ♖ac1 ♔c7 27.♗h5 e5 28.f4 ♕d6

There's Hikaru Nakamura. At the start of the baseball game between the St. Louis Cardinals and the Milwaukee Brewers, the players joined Rex Sinquefield, who was invited to throw out an honorary pitch, on the field.

29.♖f1! A strong move, and one played with very little time on the clock. It was clear that Gata had overlooked this idea.

There also was 29.♖cd1 (computers, oh the computers, they see everything) 29...exf4 30.♕f2 fxg3 31.hxg3 ♖d5 32.♗f3 ♖xd1 33.♖xd1 ♕e5 34. ♗xc6 dxc6 35.♖e1 – White is completely fine in this line as well, but with little time 29.♖f1 is far more natural.

29...exf4 30.♕xf4 ♗e4 31.♗f2

After 31.♕xd6+ ♔xd6 32.♗f3 ♔e5 White should be able to hold a draw with precise play, but Black's chances are preferable.

31...♖c3 32.♗e2

32...♔b7

A great resource is 32...♕h6!, which would have made my life difficult under time pressure. After 33.♖cd1 ♖xc2 34.♖d4 White is completely fine but I am not sure I would have been able to find this idea with 2 minutes on my clock.

33.♖cd1 ♕e6 34.♗c4 d5

35.♕c5! A strong move, and one which Gata must have missed.

35...♖d8

After 35...♕c6 36.♕xd5! ♖xc2 37.♕f7+ ♔b6 38.♖f2 ♖c3 39.♗d5, once again White is better, but there is still a lot of work to be done.

35...dxc4 runs into 36.♖d6, winning a lot of material or mating in 3 moves.

36.♕xa5 ♖xc2

37.♖f2 A bad idea was 37.♕xb4+? ♕b6+ 38.♕xb6+ ♔xb6 39.♖f2 dxc4! 40.♖xd8 ♖c1+ 41.♖f1 ♖xf1+ 42.♔xf1 cxb3 43.♔e2 b2 44.♖d1 ♔c5 and Black will bring the king over to the kingside and easily obtain a draw.

37...♖xf2 38.♕xd8 White should be winning after 38.♕xb4+?! ♕b6 39.♕xb6+ ♔xb6 40.♔xf2 ♔c5, but once again there will be a lot of work to do. Why bother?

38...♖g2+

39.♔f1 ♖b2 40.♗xd5+ ♗xd5 41.♕xd5+ ♕xd5 42.♖xd5

Gata resigned in view of 42...♖xb3 43.♖xf5 ♔c6 44.♖b5, and I will play ♔g2 next and just march my g- and h-pawns all the way up the board.

NOTES BY

Jon Ludvig Hammer

RL 18.2 – C88
Magnus Carlsen
Levon Aronian
St Louis 2013 (6)

1.e4 e5 2.♘f3 ♘c6 3.♗b5 a6 4. ♗a4 ♘f6 5.0-0 ♗e7 6.♖e1 b5 7. ♗b3 0-0 8.a4 b4 9.d4 d6 10.dxe5 dxe5 11.♕xd8

White exchanges queens, hoping to use the weakness of the c4-square to put pressure on Black's centre.

11...♖xd8 12.♘bd2 h6 13.a5 ♗c5

14.♗c4

This has become a standard manoeuvre in these positions. White is hoping to get a set-up with ♗d3, ♘c4, pawn b3 and bishop b2 – which is very harmonious and puts some serious pressure on the e5-pawn.

However, you always need to keep your opponent's ideas in mind. It might have been better to stop the knight's lunge to g4 by 14.h3.

14...♘g4 15.♖e2 ♗e6

The position is full of imbalances, and in a must-win situation (to tie for first), Aronian allows doubled pawns to exchange off White's most active piece. White is left with no development, and a headache to defend on a5.

16.♗xe6

16.♗d3 b3 causes lots of trouble – so White has to exchange.

16...fxe6 17.h3 ♘f6 18.♖e1

The computers think this is about equal, but Aronian's next couple of moves makes them change their mind. White is forced into a solid but passive defence.

18...♖ab8 19.♘c4 ♖b5 20.b3 ♗d4 21.♗b2 ♖c5

White is still solid, enjoying the holes (especially c4) Black created in his aggression. But Aronian steps up the pressure. The manoeuvre to c5 puts the rook in an excellent position, targeting a5, protecting e5 and at the same time putting pressure down the c-file. No text-book will call it an open file, but Aronian's creative play showcases its potential.

22.♖a2 ♗xb2 23.♖xb2 ♘e8 24. ♖a2 ♘d6 25.♘fd2

25...♘b7
Clearly aimed at picking up the a5-pawn, but putting that knight on c3 was arguably better, planning for total domination. Instead of tying White up, Aronian ends up struggling to untie his knight from a5 without losing the pawn behind it on a6.
26.♘f3 ♚f7 27.♚f1 ♚f6 28.♖a4 ♘bxa5 29.♘e3 h5 30.♖ea1 ♖d4

Levon Aronian was clearly struggling with his form and never got into his stride. The painful loss in the last round cost him his second place in the world rankings.

Black can afford to give up the rook, since his remaining pieces will rule the board – but there's nothing to force White to play along. Instead, Magnus manages to protect his central pawn indirectly:
31.♘e1

31...♚e7
Here 31...♖xe4 32.♘d3 ♖b5 33.c4 bxc3 34.♖xe4 is one of the most beautiful lines of the tournament, I think. There's something extraordinary about placing a second pawn in between an x-ray on a rook, knowing it can be taken by one of chess's coolest rules – only to clear the obstacles and lose the rook.
32.f3 ♖d2 33.♖d1 ♖d6 34.♖da1 ♚d7 35.♘d1 ♖d2 36.♘f2 ♚c8 37.♘fd3 ♖b5

38.h4 There's no need to be tempted to win back a pawn in the time scramble, when 38.♘xb4 ♘xb4 39.♖xa5 ♚b7 leaves Black with pressure thanks to the active rook on d2.
38...♚b7 39.♖1a2 ♚a7 40.♚g1 ♚b6 41.♚f1 g6 42.♚g1 ♚b7 43.♚f1

Going back and forth signifies the inherent solidity of White's position. Black's knights are stuck, and the only way to free them would require some protection of the a6-pawn first.
Meanwhile, a draw will secure Magnus first place, whilst Aronian needs a win for a playoff. Hence he tries to keep making progress, which now becomes the turning point of the game.
43...♚c8 44.♘f2

44...♖d8 I daresay this move cost Aronian the game. White gets to activate his pieces, and it's extremely difficult to adjust to new circumstances. The game has been very one-sided, and suddenly Black needs to play very accurately just to keep himself in the game.

45.♘ed3 ♚b7 46.♚e2 ♚b6 47.♚e3 ♚b7

Aronian offered a draw around here, but Magnus smelled blood and wanted the whole point. Magnus's image as the warrior who plays to the bitter end certainly got enhanced, but it's not just an image – it's who he is. If you consider your advantage to be risk-free, you play on, throwing up problems for your opponent, regardless of whether a draw would secure you unshared first. We can say it's admirable, but what he's doing is maximizing his chances to win games – and it's working brilliantly for him! Why change a winning strategy? Aronian collapsed in just a few moves.

48.♘d1 ♚c8 49.♘1b2 ♖d6 50. ♖a1

50...♚d8

The decisive blunder, but Black's position was already very uncomfortable.

A firm handshake sealed the end of the first Sinquefield Cup. No tiebreak, but an undisputed winner with an unambiguous final score.

50...♖d4 51.g3 ♖d7 52.f4 exf4+ 53. gxf4 ♖d8 54.♖g1 ♘d4 55.♖g2

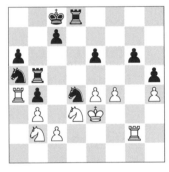

ANALYSIS DIAGRAM

opens up a new front on the kingside, and it's only a matter of time before Black's pawns start falling off.

51.♘c4 ♘xc4+ 52.bxc4 ♖b8 53.c5 ♖d7 54.♖xa6 b3 55.♖xc6 bxc2 56.♘e1 A neat move, making sure the rook on a1 is protected when the dangerous c2-pawn is captured. This wraps things up nicely – absolutely proving that Magnus was right to refuse the draw.

56...♚e7

56...♖d1 57.♘xc2 ♖xa1 58.♘xa1 ♖a8 actually wins the knight, since 59.♘c2 ♚d7 traps the rook. But White can just take on e6 instead of saving the knight – winning all the black kingside pawns.

57.♘xc2 ♖b3+ 58.♚e2 ♖b2 59. ♖c1 ♖a2 60.♚e3 ♚f7 61.f4 ♚f6 62.fxe5+ ♚xe5 63.♘e1 ♖a3+ 64.♚f2 ♖d2+ 65.♚f1 ♖d7 66. ♘f3+ ♚f4 67.♖xe6 g5 68.hxg5 ♚g3 69.♖f6 ♖a2 70.♘e5

Black resigned. ∎

St. Louis 2013				1	2	3	4	cat. XXII
								TPR
1	Magnus Carlsen	IGM NOR 2862		**	½ ½	½ 1	1 1	4½	2968
2	Hikaru Nakamura	IGM USA 2772		½ ½	**	1 0	1 ½	3½	2862
3	Levon Aronian	IGM ARM 2813		½ 0	0 1	**	½ ½	2½	2734
4	Gata Kamsky	IGM USA 2741		0 0	0 ½	½ ½	**	1½	2622

Carlsen and Son

His first attempts to win his second-born over for his favourite game did not bear fruit, but once young Magnus did fall under its spell, father Henrik kept pinching his arm. At 13, his son was a grandmaster, at 19 the number one in the world rankings, and he continues to amaze. On the eve of the World Championship match in Chennai, Henrik Carlsen talked to **Dirk Jan ten Geuzendam** about the doubts parents inevitably have, about how he and his wife on one occasion forbade their 14-year-old son to play in Mexico, about the benefits of the Norwegian school system, about the right approach to the game and about the joy of accompanying the best player on the planet on his adventures. 'This has just been a fantastic ride, very intense, a fulfilment.'

At the start of the final day of the Sinquefield Cup, the predominant mood is one of excitement fuelled by the great days behind us. But there is also regret that everything will soon be over now. No more world stars in the room upstairs, no more free food and live commentary at Lester's, no more kibitzing on the ground floor of the Club or around the chess tables outside. Why does it have to stop? As if they're gearing up to drawing up a petition, a remarkable number of visitors express their hope that there will be a nice little extra, some sweet desert after a rich meal. In other words, a tiebreak with some additional fast games.

Going by the standings, a tiebreak is not at all unlikely. Magnus Carlsen tops the table, half a point ahead of Hikaru Nakamura and a full point ahead of Levon Aronian. In the final

'Chess-wise
he's been
the boss,
all the time
basically'

round, Aronian can catch up with the leader in their direct encounter, while Nakamura faces an out-of-form Gata Kamsky. There's just one detail that spoils the prospect and suggests an entirely different scenario: both Nakamura and Aronian play with the black pieces.

Funnily enough, Henrik Carlsen tells me that Magnus had said that morning that he actually wouldn't mind a tiebreak. Of course his son had no plans to lose; he must have been thinking about a play-off with Nakamura. But some additional fireworks would be fine with him. That's all very well, I say to myself, but I don't think that either Kamsky or Carlsen will lose with white.

This conviction begins to crumble as the games get under way. Carlsen ends up in a passive position, loses a pawn and causes confusion all around. Is he losing? No, he is not. Gritting his teeth he manages to hang on and shortly before the time-control it becomes clear that there is no way for Aronian to make progress.

All along, Henrik Carlsen has been watching the game seemingly emotionlessly. He didn't show concern when his son looked to be in trouble, and doesn't seem particularly relieved now that it is clear that he will draw. Instead, with his eyes fixed on the screen, he says that now maybe Magnus wants to play for a win. A win? It almost sounds like a joke, until it becomes clear that he has excellently sensed the shift in balance in the game. Aronian offers a draw and Carlsen starts thinking. And plays on! Instead of sticking to the golden Soviet rule that you don't jeopardize tournament victory when it's up for grabs (Kamsky and Nakamura had drawn their game), he decides to go for the maximum.

I briefly think that Henrik will be shocked, but his reaction is the complete opposite. His face lights up and he is delighted. This is what he likes! He immediately adds that he himself would have taken the draw, but it's fantastic that Magnus wants to win. This is how you should play, seeing possibilities and not worrying about possible problems. With the same enthusiasm he turns to a Norwegian film crew that is here to collect material for a documentary. This is what he admires in his son. It's also the correct decision. Visibly affected by the turn of events, Aronian fails to put up the resistance that is now required and loses surprisingly quickly. Henrik is happy with Magnus's tournament victory, of course, but he is even happier with his fighting spirit. He has shown character, and that's what counts.

Whenever you talk to Henrik Carlsen about his son's achievements or his career, there is little risk that he will speak about himself. And if he does, there is a fair chance that he will explicitly state, to avoid any misunderstanding, that he doesn't want to take any credit. That's not false modesty, it's the way he is. Although he may have sparked Magnus's interest in the game and accompanied him to most of his great successes, he has not made any of the moves that led to his triumphs. For him, the past years have first and foremost been a pleasure and a privilege. An experience that he spoke about freely when we sat down for a talk at the 'Chess House', the guest house of the Saint Louis Chess Club, literally at a stone's throw from the Club.

> 'He very quickly started eating at a separate table from us, three metres away, so that he could be with the chess pieces.'

'I was introduced to chess by my parents at the age of five or six. I played a lot with my father when I was about eight years old. We even played a hundred-game match. He used to sit and think for a long time, whereas I always played very quickly and I beat him quite convincingly. Then I didn't have anyone to play with, my brother occasionally. He joined the Asker Chess Club and I followed suit. I thought that maybe I had some talent for chess, but I was surprised that in this club there were a couple of young players, who beat me soundly. Maybe I was a bit demotivated by this fact. These three young kids turned out to be Simen Agdestein and Espen Agdestein, who is now Magnus's manager, and Berge Ostenstad, who is also a grandmaster now.

'I took up chess again in 1995. I remember that I was shaking when I went to the club for an informal blitz tournament, because I hadn't played for more than 10 years. I was amazed that there was so much pressure. And I tried to teach my children. The family situation allowed it. Suddenly we felt we could do a little bit more than work, look after the children and try to survive as parents of young children usually do. Magnus and his eldest sister Ellen seemed interested. Not to the extent that they pursued it outside the few sessions that we had together. They were genuinely interested and they seemed to try, but it was just hard for them. Maybe at that point I had already read a book about the Polgars or some other prodigies that took up chess at an early age. My uncle, who was also interested in chess, told me that the son of a neighbour had picked up chess like that. Of course, I no longer believe any of these stories about kids immediately understanding chess. Magnus and Ellen learned the rules quickly, they could capture pieces quite soon, but making two or more pieces work together... that they simply couldn't handle. I quickly thought that chess was not for them. One of the challenges when you play

Magnus and Henrik Carlsen on their way to the Saint Louis Chess Club for the fifth round of the Sinquefield Cup.

with small children is that on the one hand you don't want to give them false beliefs in the sense that they can expect their opponents to blunder a piece on every move, but on the other hand you cannot beat them all the time. So at first we struggled; how do we play together? When Magnus was six or so, I would start with a king and one pawn and he would have all his pieces and pawns. And then he would beat me. Or stalemate me! But in any case I would not beat him with the pawn, he would capture it.

'It was typically an activity we did in the autumn, when it's raining. We didn't put any special emphasis on chess until close before Magnus turned eight. In the autumn of 1998, I played a bit with Ellen, and then she understood that she also had to make it a little bit interesting for me. We then reached the point where Ellen and I could play a game. Of course I could beat her if I wanted to, but she started

to think. We played a few games and then Magnus started to watch. And then he very quickly started to sit on his own with his chess set. And he very quickly started eating at a separate table from us, three metres away, so that he could be with the chess pieces. You know, Norwegian upbringing is very relaxed. Children normally do what they want. Magnus already had a record for doing things while we were eating anyway. Reading one of his books, or making a puzzle, and now he wanted to move his chess pieces. I watched and saw that he would repeat something that he had seen when I was playing with his sister, or he would repeat something that we had looked at or played in a game.

He would play games against himself, playing both sides. And then at a certain point he would like the white position and he would allow a nice mate by White. He really spent a lot of time at the board that winter. After a couple of months the belief returned that I had had originally in 1995, that maybe chess was something for him, based on his other abilities. But the good thing was that I had not put any emphasis on chess for years. Now it was his thing. I hadn't pushed him. At some point I said, well, if you're this interested, we can play the Norwegian championship this summer. I can play in the adult section and you can play Under-11, and we can all go on a family vacation. The championship took place in Gausdal, a nice place to go for walks and play tennis, go swimming. And he really liked that idea. That was his first tournament.

'I think most parents are looking for something in their children. When

Magnus was three or four – his sister was one year older – I thought to myself, these kids are probably not geniuses in any way, but it doesn't matter. I love them! From that moment onwards the focus was not on what these kids could do. Before you have children you think of these things, but then at one point you realize that it doesn't matter. Then other people pointed at some of his traits that were kind of special. That he could concentrate for a long time, maybe hours at a time, at a very early age. He was very interested in certain topics; cars when he was two, puzzles for a couple of years from when he was one and a half, other countries, municipalities, information about this. He knew an enormous amount of sports results when he was six, seven years old. He was reading these sports results books. Frankly, I thought this was normal. I didn't have any comparisons. Except he had a cousin who read much more than Magnus. His sisters are also quite bright, so to me it was normal. His memory was good, but whether it was exceptional, I don't know. Still, when he was about five, I told my wife that with his traits he could become a good chess player. But it completely left my mind for four years. And when he picked it up and became competitive, my ambitions were gone. It was his stuff. That was important. I could well imagine that I could have killed his interest by being too eager, too pushy. Of course it may have encouraged him to feel that I liked it. I did, of course. I thought it was great. And he got prac-

tical support, he was allowed to play a lot. But I can really say, we didn't push him in any way. And it wouldn't have worked.'

More and more time was spent on chess, and he was getting better and better. Were you happy that he liked chess so much, or also worried that it might become an obsession?
'I spent a lot of time and energy thinking about this, maybe from when he was nine and a half till he was 13, 14, 15. Let me start with my wife; she's not a chess player. At one of the tournaments in Gausdal, in the summer of 2000, she was watching him play and she said, "It looks like he is suffering. I want to take him under my arm and bring him home. It looks painful sitting there for hours, thinking." And she asked him after the game: was it painful? And he looked at her astonished, he didn't understand at all. And I explained to her that chess players are extending themselves, they are putting an effort in this. You may have facial expressions that don't have anything to do with pain or displeasure. That relieved her, that she need not worry.

'We were also happy that besides chess he played a lot of football, did

a lot of sports in general. And he was doing well in school. When he started in the first grade he was very good at maths.

'As for me, I was thinking about this as well. What is best for him? What is the purpose of life? Is it to be happy? Is it to exploit your talents? Are those commensurate values? These kinds of philosophical questions. Frankly, I felt early on that if he had a talent for

> 'Frankly, I felt early on that if he had a talent for this and an interest in it, it would be unfair to stop him.'

this and an interest in it, it would be unfair to stop him. Unless for health reasons. Even if it would interfere slightly with his school. So, how much should we encourage him? We encouraged him, indirectly, through practical support. Going to tournaments with him. I remember when he was 10, 11; we would go through Harmen Jonkman's website calendar of chess tournaments and it was like being in a candy store.

'And then you had these concerns about him playing so much against adults, spending so much time outside his normal social environment. But these fears were alleviated by the fact that two of his sisters also played chess. They moved in several social groups. Music, horses, dancing. But in a way they seemed to prefer the chess environment, because they found

people friendly and natural, not artificial or pretentious. They felt at ease and felt that it was a meaningful social environment.'

Norway was not a real chess country. How did your family and friends react?
'My parents, they were not concerned. They watch their grandchildren and they like it if they have special interests, go their own way. They like characters! They saw characters in all their grandchildren and thought it was great. My wife's father went to a couple of tournaments with Magnus when I couldn't go. And he enjoyed it a lot.

'As for other people in Norway... At school the headmaster said that he was doing OK. She never turned down an application for something meaningful. She thought the balance between school and other activities was very important. She was always very cooperative. This was our choice. If you were to mention factors contributing to Magnus's possibilities to use his talents, you'd have to name the Norwegian school system. And the Internet. The possibility to play online starting from the late 1990s. He spent a lot of time on ICC and later Playchess. He made a lot of progress that way. I just loved watching it, sitting at my own computer and wondering, how can he play like this? He is 10 or 11!'

When Magnus decided to quit school he was already a very strong player. Yet you must have worried whether this was the right path to follow.
'Yeah, but that was such a gradual process. When he was between 12 and 15, we continually said to other people and in discussions with him that his chess hobby was fantastic, but that it would probably be good to have a balance in life. We think you should have an education parallel to chess and later you can choose what to do. But by the time he started high school we felt that, one, he is making his own decisions, two, we have repeated this to the point where we feel that he knows what we feel and think, and is capa-

Physical exercise and outdoor activities have always been important. When Magnus Carlsen made his debut in Wijk aan Zee, in 2004, he would often play football with his father on the village green in the morning.

ble of making decisions on his own. I think that when he was 15, we already saw it coming that he really wanted to be a chess player. People around him like Kasparov or Vladimirov wrote about him in your magazine, saying that of course he could be a top chess player if he wanted.

'When he started high school, he liked it a lot for a few months, but then gradually his interest waned and in the second year, in one of the semesters, he was away for chess tournaments 70 per cent of the time. And that made it very hard for him to catch up. Typically then, when he came home from a chess tournament he was tired, and then he would have to get up early the next morning to go to school. School interested him less and less and he started regarding it as just a nuisance. At some point he went there and the teacher told him what to do to finish, but he didn't care. He wanted to play chess, to use his energy for his chess career, doing his best.'

At the same time you were developing into a father who usually accompanied him to tournaments. How did you feel about this? As if you were in a candy

store, or did you also have doubts: should I do this instead of pursuing my own professional ambitions?
'I was having thoughts like that, yes. I worked in the oil industry until 2001. I was an engineer with Exxon, and then I started as an independent IT consultant, mainly for the oil industry. This was convenient, but it was not the reason I went to work part-time. I could not start to base my life on his chess activities, no way. In 2006 he started his company, Magnus Chess. He was beginning to make money. We had a discussion with the tax authorities and from 2006 they said, now it's probably reasonable that he pays taxes. We know you had costs and he had income, but now obviously he is making money. We started a company to make it all transparent, with an auditor, and he put his chess activities into the company. At that point I still worked a lot as a consultant, but frankly I preferred going to chess tournaments. I found that this was probably the best job I could have. I could follow the games, which is a pastime for others, but for me it had the added benefit that I would be able to talk to Magnus about the game afterwards.

Going to tournaments and bringing one or two of his sisters, I enjoyed it very much. Last year I did some consultancy work again, this year I am just trying to enjoy this special year with the World Championship, helping out a bit. When I am at home my wife is happy. If I make dinner, she will not complain about anything. I don't have to, but if I do, she's happy.'

When I see you follow the games, I never see you overly excited or carried away. Are you hiding your emotions carefully?
'Well, thank you! Of course it can be exciting. I could well imagine that if he had struggled more in his chess career, following all his games would have been much harder. Of course I've been spoiled, there have been successes all the way. I told myself when he was 13, wow, so he has chess talent, he is a grandmaster! What happened? This is his hobby, and it should continue to be so. If he stops tomorrow, that would be fine. I am not going to expect anything more in any way. If he achieves anything more it will be a bonus. And these bonuses kept on coming.'

There was this dramatic moment in the London Candidates' tournament when he lost to Ivanchuk and it very much looked as if this world championship dream was going to be blown to shreds for the moment. How did you take that blow?
'One comment on that. I do not agree that it looked bleak. Because it's the wrong attitude to it in a way. I mean, there are only opportunities in chess.

I agree that his opportunities were slightly fewer after the game against Ivanchuk than they had been before. But still he was back on the attack, where he loves to be.'

When you looked at it objectively, things didn't look that good.
'When I went over to the playing hall together with Peter Heine Nielsen, I think the last thing we had seen in the hotel was that he had saved the position. He had tricked Ivanchuk with this h4 manoeuvre or something. And then it was a draw again. We understood it was still difficult, but we went over and then he had blundered and lost. Of course, I would have preferred him not to, but it's not my...'

Were you taking it that philosophically? If he doesn't win then he doesn't win?
'How else should I take it?'

As many sports fans do, particularly if it's someone this close to you; just feel bad.
'Yeah, but if you feel bad and you're an adult you either have to do something about it or accept it… I mean, behave yourself (laughs).'

You didn't even feel bad for a moment?
'(Sighs) What do you mean by bad? Of course, in one sense...'

Lying in bed and thinking, wouldn't it be a shame if he didn't win, being so close…
'Well, you have a point. I think I have some of the same emotions on this

as Magnus himself. And normally the emphasis is always on the possibilities. You don't think that there is something to lose. There is nothing to lose, because you basically have nothing. But there's something to win. And this focus is what Magnus has been very good at. At some point during the Candidates', as has appeared from interviews, the comments he has made himself, he certainly thought that the Candidates' was his to lose. He was leading after 11 rounds and he made these mistakes against Ivanchuk, and Ivanchuk played very well and suddenly he started worrying about not winning the event. And that's the wrong focus. But I understand him, I had similar feelings. You're ranked number one by far and if you can't win the Candidates', you're far away from the match and the World Championship title. And it's not commensurate with your rating status, to be that far away. In that sense he felt a lot of pressure in the last three rounds. And I understood and felt some of the same, although, again, it's not my business; I am a spectator. I had a holiday in London, in a nice hotel, with my family, what more can I ask for?'

If he wins, you're happy; if he doesn't win you're not unhappy.
'(Emphatically) I shouldn't be, definitely. I mean, I have no reason to be unhappy about that. And that's very important to me.'

At some point Magnus said, 'As long as it's theoretically possible that I can win I believe that I will win.' Is that him or is that also some of you?

'That's him. But I understand him and I appreciate that idea. Somehow you have to focus on a broader basis than just the result. The result of the game shouldn't matter, the game itself brings opportunities for winning tournaments. It's his idea, but I very much understand what he is saying. And I love to hear him say it. It's the right approach.'

At first you accompanied him as his father. Of course, you're still his father, but undoubtedly your relationship has developed. Are you still very much the father or are you more of a buddy?

'I think it was a bit difficult when I was his manager. And the managerial role was important. We got some help from Espen Agdestein finding sponsors back in 2009. He helped us secure sponsorship for the Kasparov cooperation. And Magnus rose to number one in the rankings. At that point it was a bit difficult to combine being father and manager. So in early 2011 I suggested to Magnus that since Espen had shown that he could get sponsors, maybe we should let him be manager as well? We were working very well with him. And Magnus agreed to that and that helped in a way. Because now, for two and a half years, I have been back to being father, support person, pal. And you may say, father and pal, that's so different. No, it's much more the same than being the manager. As a manager you have to ask him all these questions and kind of negotiate between him and the organizers and media. And I wanted to say yes to both. And the media and organizers expected more from me, because I was the father and could also influence him, while Magnus expected more from me than from a professional manager. You're my father, you should defend me, help me. So I felt a bit under attack from two sides. Now that Espen is doing it and there are difficult decisions, I say, well you have to talk to Espen. Of

course Espen and I also talk, but in the end I don't have to take decisions and choose between the interests of my son and other parties.'

You didn't like your role as manager. That reminds me of some moments when you didn't want to interfere with decisions of his, saying, 'So far he's always been right'.

'How to improve his chess. Magnus has on a couple of occasions taken decisions that I doubted were the best decisions for him at the time. But I didn't interfere; I even tried not to show my feelings. Because up to when he was 16, 17, it was a hobby, and later he's always shown that he knows what he is doing. So I just let it go. It's your decision.

We had a discussion about whether he played too much when he was in his early teens. For his health, a balance in life, et cetera. On one occasion we said to Magnus that he could not go to Mexico. That would be the third tournament in a row. You'll never be at school. You will be so tired, why not spend some time in Norway? Go skiing. And he said, no, I want to go to Mexico. And we said, no, it's too much for you. And he said, OK. But even two years later he would say, 'I remember you stopped me from going to Mexico. And I still don't agree.' He was maybe 14. That was the last time... We still felt that we knew what was best for him, but after that we also thought, he probably knows what he is doing. It seems that way.

'We talk about things. Of course, indirectly parents influence their children, even if you don't tell them what to do. You try to give values, ideas, perspectives. But chess-wise he's basically been the boss all the time. Maybe especially so since he became a grand-

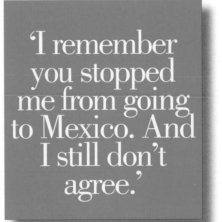

'I remember you stopped me from going to Mexico. And I still don't agree.'

master; that boosted his confidence even more.'

You've witnessed almost all his successes. Which of them delighted you most?

'Of course, his successes have become more important in a sense. But that would mean that I appreciate what he is doing now more than what he did 10 years ago. If he loses, it's more serious as well. And I don't want that. This is just a game. OK, it's his work. But he is doing fine, he has money. The essence is that it's a game, that he is enjoying it. In that sense it meant just as much when he was achieving something long ago. I thought that when he became U-11 champion at nine and a half, that was great. Some of the Norwegian players present were saying such nice things about him. I overheard Kjetil Lie saying, (as if in awe) he's going to be incredibly good. Jøran Aulin-Jansson, the president of the Norwegian chess federation, said, "This is the biggest talent I have seen since at least Simen Agdestein and maybe ever in Norway."

'At that point I didn't have many expectations. Magnus was interested, but we hadn't seen much. He was winning the U-11 at nine and a half, but compared to Karjakin, Nepomniachtchi or McShane he was a beginner. They already were masters at eight and a half. Only two and a half years later he was catching up with these guys. So I think those moments when he did something you didn't expect at all, that was extremely fascinating. He can still amaze. Like the tournament in London in December, the tournament in Wijk aan Zee in January, where he went with little preparation, wanting to enjoy himself, and still scored the best result ever. The same as Kasparov, plus seven with 13 rounds. It's mind-boggling in a way, how can this happen? He's continued to amaze, but of course it gets harder for him now. He is the number 1 and he hasn't had a bad tournament since the Olympiad in 2010. Well, strike that, because I think he never has a bad tournament by definition. He is doing so well. But relative to his other performances the Olympiad 2010 was quite mediocre for him. He has had three years now with only first and second places.'

Magnus has never said that the world championship is his ultimate goal. Yet you must feel that he is close to realizing a big dream, probably also one of your dreams. How big was or is this dream?
'He's reached the number one spot in the ratings, he's won a lot of tournaments over the past four, five years, so in a way it's a natural challenge available in the chess world. At the same time, objectively, people are putting too much emphasis on the world championship, especially now that they play just 12 games, the qualification cycles, the way they are. Objectively speaking, the tradition is strong. Anand has proven himself by winning several matches, but the process is in no way perfect. It's not obvious that the best player in the world, by most standards, will be the World Champion. You could turn it around and say, well, by definition the World Champion is the best player in the world. These are semantics in a way. If you are on the opposite side of this argument, you will never agree. In chess the tradition is that the champion is the king in a way, with the privileges and everything. I think this affects Magnus in the sense that people care so much about this title, so he thinks, let me take it as well.

'Where he is landing on this I am not quite sure. But the good thing is that while nearly three years ago he opted out of the Candidates' in Kazan, because he didn't feel properly motivated for the whole process, now he's been saying for a year, "I really want to play Anand in a match." And it's

coming from inside. And I am happy about this, because he wants to do it and then by definition it's the right thing, whether he will win or not. I also think that if he continues to play chess for many years, if he doesn't win against Anand this year, it will still be a valuable experience which will make it much easier to come back. Both to play the qualifications and play a future match. You've been there, seen it, learned from it.'

Probably it's not the patience he has at the moment.
'No. He shouldn't think like that. As he said, "I need to believe that I will win the match." That's the approach.'

Do you give much thought to what he may do after his chess career?
'Occasionally, but less and less, because he seems capable of finding areas that he can drive into and become interested in. He's following the news quite closely. He's starting to understand a bit more about international politics, economics, business. I think his chess career prepares him to become a high achiever in whatever he wants to pursue. He knows now more or less what it takes. And even though he has not really struggled to get there, he's put in a lot of hours. People say he is lazy, but he's probably spent as much time on chess as any 22-year-old in history. I would guess. Maybe I am wrong, but it's probably close. He's spent a lot of time on chess.
And it's not my business. I cannot have any ambitions for him, especially not beyond chess. I should start with myself...'

Yes, what will it do to you, suppose...
'That he stops playing chess? Well, I

can take a deep breath and go back to a life where chess is not as important and in a way that's an opportunity as well. I am not asking for that opportunity now, because I like the chess world, but in that sense I am not worrying. This has just been a fantastic ride, very intense, a fulfilment. I mean, I am so happy about following chess, being part of the chess world. There are so many fascinating people.
No, I don't fear that moment at all. You see, I had four small children and a lot of work at some point. After that experience I am never going to be bored. I can do nothing, but I will not be bored. For the last 15 to 20 years I cannot remember any moment of being bored. And I cannot foresee that in the future either.'

All these years you spent in the chess world, have they changed your views on the merits of chess for society?
'I am not sure that's my call. But it's also a question I'd like to answer, because I truly believe that playing some chess is a blessing for youngsters. Because simply analytically speaking, what you want to do with a child is to help it train the faculties needed for learning, thinking, analysing, making decisions. And chess is a game made for luring children into training these abilities. Objectively speaking, that must be the case, I strongly believe that. Whether it is time better spent than working on your maths or your music or other interests you might have, I don't know. But if you have a child doing something really meaningless, I think, playing some chess must be a blessing. In that sense chess has an important role to play in the world and I am very happy if Magnus and I, as a helper, can support this.' ∎

> '**I think his chess career prepares him to become a high achiever in whatever he wants to pursue.**'

FINALLY!
THE COMPLETE ENGLISH EDITION OF THE ACCLAIMED CLASSIC!

J.H.DONNER

THE KING
CHESS PIECES

During the entire month of November

FREE!

All non-subscription orders above €50/$60 will receive a free copy of this magnificent 392 pages book!

The King
Chess Pieces
by J.H. Donner
New In Chess, 2006, 392 pages

~~$29.95~~ ~~€27.95~~ **FREE**

The King is probably the best book we ever published. J.H.Donner (1927-1988) was a Dutch Grandmaster and one of the greatest writers about chess of all time. He was a chess reporter and a chess columnist, as well as an annotator of the game. Above all he was a witty and unpredictable commentator of everything and everybody, both inside and outside the chess world.

"Far and away the finest chess writing ever seen. Trust me, you don't want to be without this book."
Jeremy Silman, author of 'How to Reasses Your Chess'

"A work that all chess players should own. It would probably be my only 'desert island' chess book."
John Saunders, British Chess Magazine

"The book has blown me away. I am raving about it to all my friends!"
Fred Waitzkin, author of 'Searching for Bobby Fischer'

100 Endgames You Must Know
Third, Improved and Extended Edition
by Jesus De la Villa Garcia
New In Chess, 2012, 256 pages

€21.95

A Practical White Repertoire with 1.d4 and 2.c4
Volume 1: The Complete Queen's Gambit
by Alexei Kornev
Chess Stars, 2013, 304 pages

€21.95

Best Play
A New Method to Find the Strongest Move
by Alexander Shashin
Mongoose Press, 2013, 404 pages

€24.95

Chess Legends: Move by Move
Learn from the games of Capablanca, Botvinnik & Kramnik
by Cyrus Lakdawala
Everyman Chess, 2013, 1184 pages
3 volumes

~~€73.85~~ **€64.95**

Sacrifice and Initiative in Chess
Seize the Moment to Get the Advantage
by Ivan Sokolov
New In Chess, 2013, 256 pages

€24.95

Steamrolling the Sicilian
Play for a Win with 5.f3!
by Sergey Kasparov
New In Chess, 2013, 240 pages
NEW!

€23.95

Complete Slav I & II
Save 10% on both books combined
by Konstantin Sakaev
Chess Evolution, 2013, 676 pages
2 volumes

~~€49.90~~ **€44.95**

ChessBase 12 Starter / Mega / Premium Package
Wissen Ist Matt
by The ChessBase team
ChessBase, 2012, DVD-ROM

€179.90

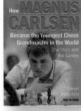

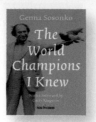

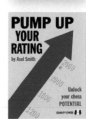

NOVEMBER SPECIAL
NEW IN CHESS ONLINE SHOP

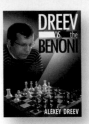

Dreev vs. the Benoni
The Best Move Orders for White
by Alexey Dreev
Chess Stars, 2013, 268 pages

€20.95

Grandmaster Repertoire 14 - The French Defence
Volume 1 - The Winawer Variation
by Emanuel Berg
Quality Chess, 2013, 328 pages
NEW!

€24.95

A Cunning Chess Opening Repertoire for White
A Flexible Repertoire to take your opponents out of their comfort zone
by Graham Burgess
Gambit, 2013, 192 pages
NEW!

€20.25

DGT Bluetooth/USB e-Board Rosewood Timeless
DGT projects, 2010, Chess Board: Rosewood
Chess Pieces: Timeless Pieces

~~€674.00~~ €595.00

#4
SPECIAL
DISCOUNT
SAVE
60%

Tactimania
Find the Winning Combination
by Glenn Flear
Quality Chess, 2011, 264 pages

~~€21.95~~ €8.75

Don't be deceived by the strange title and the silly cover! This is NOT your run-of-the-mill fairy tale with chess moves, for kids. It is an extremely valuable tactics training book with hundreds of to-the-point exercises which we guarantee that you have never seen before. For improving chess players up to candidate-masters. Only during November available at a 60% discount.

The King's Gambit
A Grandmaster Guide
by John Shaw
Quality Chess, 2013, 680 pages
NEW!

€24.95

The Magic Tactics of Mikhail Tal
Learn from the Legend
by Karsten Müller, Raymund Stolze
New In Chess, 2012, 334 pages

€24.95

Mastering Strategy Series
Save 10% on the Complete Series
by Johan Hellsten
Everyman Chess, 2012, 1408 pages
3 volumes: Endgame, Opening and Chess Strategy

~~€77.85~~ €69.95

Platonov's Chess Academy
Using Soviet-era methods to improve 21st-century openings
by Lev Alburt & Sam Palatnik
CIRC, 2012, 176 pages

€27.95

Winning with the Najdorf Sicilian
An Uncompromising Repertoire for Black
by Zaven Andriasyan
New In Chess, 2013, 256 pages

€24.95

FREE with all non-subscription orders above €50/$60 during November 2013

'Now that I am here I might as well try to win it'

PHOTOS ALEXANDER MOTYLEV

He never much liked the knock-out format, but this time he had no choice. A new stipulation in the rules forced Vladimir Kramnik to take part in the FIDE World Cup in Tromsø if he wanted to qualify for the 2014 Candidates'. Initially he said he didn't mind an early elimination, but once he warmed up he must have started thinking what many were thinking: who was going to knock him out? Fully focused and sticking to a strict daily routine, the Russian favourite cleared one obstacle after the other to claim a supreme victory. In the slipstream of Kramnik's rout Dmitry Andreikin and Sergey Karjakin completed the euphoria in the Russian camp by claiming two further spots in the Candidates'. **Simen Agdestein** reports on another international highlight on Norwegian soil.

The World Cup in Tromsø, a huge event that the organizers of the 2014 Olympiad were not quite aware of that they had to organize as part of the Olympic bid – was another thrill for Norwegian Chess. This spring we had Norway Chess with all the best players in the world, but then there was room for only 10 players. This time there were 128!

FIDE had made sure that the best had to play if they wanted to qualify for the next Candidates' tournament. Two spots in that tournament are accorded by rating, and those would go to Vladimir Kramnik and Levon Aronian – provided they play in the World Cup (or the Grand Prix, for that matter, but that was no longer possible). As Kramnik, with his win in the Tromsø World Cup, actually qualified for a second time, he cleared the way to the Candidates' for his countryman Sergey Karjakin, who was the next in line based on the average of his recent ratings.

However, for most of the players in the FIDE World Cup, qualifying for the Candidates' wasn't the issue. It was rather about money! A lot was at stake. First prize was 120,000 dollars, but even for those knocked out in the first round there was a consolation prize of 6,000. But, mind you, in both cases the 20 per cent FIDE tax and all expenses had to be deducted.

The focus in Tromsø is very much

on the Olympiad next year. At that event there will be 1,500 players and perhaps a total of 5,000 people to handle. However, the World Cup is also a great event in itself, and I wish the Norwegian press had realized what a fantastic show there was on at the Scandic Hotel for three weeks running.

Every match was a huge battle, not only for the players, but also for the many followers on the Internet. The transmission of the games has really become brilliant. Not only are all the games shown live with computer analysis under every board, there is also live commentary by experts who try to highlight all the critical moments and entertain the online audience.

Following everything was a hard job. Already in the first round there was great excitement in most matches, but where to focus when you have 64 games taking part at the same time? As a spectator you were almost relieved when the field got smaller as players were knocked out. After all, it doesn't take a lot of players to make a great show and provide wonderful entertainment. Initially there was so much that it sometimes felt like an overload.

I myself, at least, made sure not to add to the confusion by seeing to it that nothing exciting happened in my first encounter. Norway, as the organizer, had four spots in the Cup, and those were highly appreciated, as it's not easy to qualify by ordinary means.

We knew who we would meet in the first round a month in advance, which gave us plenty of time to prepare. I wouldn't say we used that time very well, but at least it inspired us to look at chess with a clear goal in mind. I was facing Etienne Bacrot, the French number one before the tournament, but no longer so after the last round, as Maxime Vachier-Lagrave made a huge leap during this Cup. For an amateur like me, preparing for a world-class player like Bacrot was very interesting. Bacrot had already played almost 100 games this year and

Jon Ludvig Hammer had a good time. The Norwegian number two knocked out Sergei Movsesian and David Navara (l.) before he succumbed to Gata Kamsky in Round 3.

he is a full professional. Just before the World Cup I had played a tournament in Barcelona and had even won it with 8½ of 9, which was nice, but the

days when I competed with the very best in the world go back more than 25 years. I certainly could do with a little more practice. However, what happened in my first game was really embarrassing.

KI 26.6 – E73
Simen Agdestein
Etienne Bacrot
Tromsø 2013 (1.1)

1.d4 ♘f6 2.c4 g6 3.♘c3 ♗g7 4.e4 d6 5.♗e2 0-0 6.♗g5 ♘a6 7.♕d2 c6 8.♘f3 e5 9.0-0 exd4 10.♘xd4 ♘c5

'The Norwegian press is not really interested in chess, in case you thought so. They are interested in Magnus!'

I had looked at this position the day before and I thought I knew that 11. ♗f3 was the main line, which it's not. It is 11.♕f4 with interesting play, because it's not so easy for Black to get out of the queen and bishop battery on the kingside. But then I thought: why not simply play 11.f3 and get a good version of a familiar structure? **11.f3?? ♘fxe4!** That was it for me! A month of preparation and weeks and days of tension just down the drain almost before it all started. There are no tricks and White is just having a horrible position in all lines. After **12.♘xe4 ♘xe4 13.fxe4 ♗xd4+ 14.♕xd4 ♕xg5 15.♕xd6 ♖d8 16.♕a3 ♖d2** it took only 27 moves before I could resign.

The other Norwegians did slightly better, but three of us were easily knocked out after the two first games. Fortunately, Jon Ludvig Hammer, the fourth and highest rated, managed to beat both Sergei Movsesian and David Navara, but had to succumb to Gata Kamsky in Round 3.

So, performance-wise, we take our share of the responsibility why almost nobody on the street in Tromsø knew that there was a fantastic event going on in the neighbourhood. The fact that Magnus Carlsen was not there was also a reason. The Norwegian press is not really interested in chess, in case you thought so. They are interested in Magnus! A job has to be done there, as there actually were lots of wonderful stories in this World Cup. And excitement and sensations is what any sports fanatic looks for.

Julio Granda Zuniga is the first name that comes to mind. This Peruvian Grandmaster is really an impressive figure. He is of my age, which is almost half a century, and I remember him with a high rating even back in the good old junior days. At the time he was rated far higher than players like Anand and Ivanchuk, for instance. Coming from Peru. Really impressive!

He still maintains a rating as high as 2664. These days he impresses by his ostensibly total lack of knowledge of opening theory. 'So much theory!' he says, shaking his head. I wonder if he even has a computer. You wouldn't think so when you look at his games, but still – he managed to beat world-class players like Hrant Melkumyan, Peter Leko and Anish Giri before he finally had to throw in the towel against Fabiano Caruana. Even Garry Kasparov praised Granda for his sound positional chess.

Evgeny Tomashevsky, age 26, also relaunched himself in this tournament. The 13th World Champion commented that some of the players in this cup got far because of their fighting skills and some for their chess skills. Of course, they are all strong players, but following Tomashevsky was basically watching a tremendous fighting performance. Especially nerve-wracking was his encounter with Alexander Morozevich in Round 4.

After two draws in the ordinary games and then two draws in the rapid games with 25 minutes each and a 10-second increment per move, the excitement started in the first game with 10 minutes and 10-second increments:

Tomashevsky-Morozevich
Tromsø 2013 (4.5)
position after 28...♗e5

Tomashevsky has been two pawns up for a while and is still completely winning, but look what happened! **29.♕d5?** ♗xb2 There was no need to give away that pawn. **30.♘d4 ♘f6 31.♕b3?!** 31.♕e5 is better, but things have become complicated. **31...♗xd4 32.exd4 ♘e4 33.♕d5 ♖d8 34.♖c1 ♕xa4** Suddenly the material is balanced and it's White who's under pressure.

35.♕f7+? 35.♕b7+ and taking on b6 maintains the balance. **35...♔h6 36.♕e7?** Tomashevsky has lost his head, but it wasn't so easy. **36...♕xb4 0-1** 37.♕xd8 ♕xd4+ is mate.

In the next game with the same time-control Tomashevsky managed to squeeze out a win from a completely equal position. It took 169 moves and

A unique talent. Peru's Julio Granda eliminated Hrant Melkumyan, Peter Leko and Anish Giri, before he finally had to throw in the towel against Fabiano Caruana.

more than an hour of play with the clock constantly ticking close to zero. I was one of the many people biting their nails as we followed this live on the Net. In the blitz games after this tremendous struggle, Morozevich naturally seemed exhausted, while Tomashevsky kept his full energy and won the first game and actually took a draw in the second rather than mating in one. He only saw it when he repeated the position and his opponent offered a draw!

Tomashevsky had a similar fight against Alejandro Ramirez in the first round. Then it took nine games and the match was finally decided in the Armageddon game.

Beating Levon Aronian in Round 3 somehow went more smoothly:

NOTES BY
Evgeny Tomashevsky

SL 1.3 – D30
Levon Aronian
Evgeny Tomashevsky
Tromsø 2013 (3.1)

'One of the most important wins in my career so far' – at the press conference immediately afterwards, that was how I characterized the first game of my third round match of the World Cup in Tromsø against Levon Aronian. But even now, when the emotions have calmed down somewhat, I can confirm this assessment. In principle, for its justification the very fact is sufficient – it is not every day that one is able to defeat such an outstanding player, and with the black pieces. But here I was also able to demonstrate a fair standard of play, after employing an opening that was almost new for me, and to overcome an important psychological barrier (about which, see below). To be fair, the success was considerably aided, apart from my own efforts, by other factors. Thus during our match Aronian looked a little 'out of

sorts' and unwell, which was probably reflected in his play. Also in my favour was the psychological background to the game: Levon needed to confirm his status as favourite not only in the match, but also in the Cup as a whole, whereas I had practically nothing to lose after the tournament grid was published ☺, and especially when, after I had been losing 3-4 before the eighth game of my first round match with the emboldened Alejandro Ramirez, any game in the subsequent rounds was perceived as a bonus! This unusual combination of circumstances enabled me, finally, to feel liberated, put many preparations into effect and for the first time in a long period to solve the 'riddle' of good play and excellent result.

1.d4 d5 2.c4 e6 3.♘f3 c6
It was only during the afore-mentioned first round match that I played this for the first time. In the fifth game this move order brought me quite a good win, but in the seventh game it produced a heavy defeat, so that the emotional background before the full debut of the 'triangle' in my 'classical' practice was mixed ☺.

4.e3 Levon chooses the simplest and safest continuation, inviting Black to go in for Meran positions or to set up a 'Stonewall'. I was in fact aiming for this set-up, which in general has a rather dubious reputation, but in the given version is considered comparatively acceptable. The resulting positions are rather complicated and relatively unexplored. Besides, you should not be afraid of playing the 'wall' if for several years your trainer and second has been grandmaster Alexey Ilyushin, one of the most fervent supporters of the 'Stonewall'. If you look at his games and listen to, so to speak, his ideological justification for Black's play in the given scheme, you sometimes gain the feeling that only against 1.e4 is it not worth erecting the 'wall'... ☺ And although I do not experience such optimism on seeing the c6-d5-e6-f5 pawn chain, there were some ideas that I wanted to try.

4...♗d6 5.♗d3 f5 6.0-0 ♘f6 7.b3 ♕e7 8.♘e5
The main line is considered to be 8.♗b2 0-0 9.♕c1, but it is hard to understand in what way the simple and sensible text set-up is any worse.
8...0-0 9.♗b2 ♗d7!?
This typical manoeuvre of the light-squared bishop without weakening the queenside was what Alexey and I had devised. Black wants to create a set-up which is as flexible as possible without the formation of additional weaknesses.
10.♘c3 ♗e8 At this point it is appropriate to quote the tweet of my good friend, great humourist, grandmaster and public figure Alexander Evdokimov, which appeared after the game: 'I see that Tomashevsky won. Bishop on e8, Stonewall set-up. One senses the influence of the trainer.' Fortunately, the game concluded with a positive result for me, otherwise there would have been more such 'jokes' and they would have been of a less friendly nature... ☺

11.cxd5?! This first questionable (or in my view, altogether poor) decision is a reason for switching, at last, to actual chess commentary. This exchange is normally good in cases when the black knight has already come out to d7 and/or the pawn has moved to b6. Then in this way White can count on achieving slight but comfortable pressure. But here the knight is conveniently developed on the defended c6-square, there is nothing concrete to latch onto on the queenside, and Black effectively solves his opening problems. I think that 11.♖c1 or 11.♘e2 is more critical – this is a platform for future discussions.

11...cxd5

12.♖c1 The natural continuation. Little is promised by the immediate 12.♘b5 ♗xb5 (here there is no point in playing 12...♗b4 13.♕c2! ♗xb5 – 13...♘c6 14.a3 ♗a5 15.♕c5! – 14.♗xb5 a6 15.♗d3) 13.♗xb5 ♘bd7, when after ...a7-a6 followed by ...♗a3 Black has no particular problems, while the typical manoeuvre 12.♘e2 ♘c6 13.♘f4, apart from anything else, now involves a problematic pawn sacrifice: 13...♗xe5 14.dxe5 ♘g4 15.a4 a5, with counterplay.

12...♘c6 13.♘b5 ♗b4 At first sight Black loses time with this bishop, but to disturb it White also disrupts the coordination of his pieces.

14.a3

14.f3!? a6 15.♘c3 was probably somewhat more subtle – without the knight advance to e4 it is more difficult for Black to develop his forces, and the immediate exchange on e5 may lead to a strategically unpleasant position.

14...♗a5

15.♗e2 A subtle move – White vacates the excellent d3-point for his

Evgeny Tomashevsky on his decision to decline Levon Aronian's draw offer: 'If you don't continue in such a position, why play chess at all?'

knight, at the same time taking control of the important squares h5 and g4.

15...a6

15...♘e4 16.b4 a6 looks questionable. I preferred to play more simply.

16.♘c3 ♘e4 17.b4

If White does not want to immediately 'sound the retreat' with 17.♘xe4 fxe4 18.f4, then practically the only worthy alternative to the move in the game is the pawn sacrifice 17.♘d3 ♗xc3 18. ♗xc3 ♘xc3 19.♖xc3 ♕xa3 20.♘c5, but I do not think that White's compensation allows him to hope for more than equality, for example: 20...♕b4 21.♕d2 ♘d8 intending ♗b5.

17...♗c7 Black has achieved a harmonious arrangement of his pieces.

18.♘xe4 A turning-point in the game. In itself this is more of an inaccuracy than a mistake, but it is the start of a series of minor errors by White, the reason for which were, I think, mainly psychological. White should have admitted that he had no advantage, and either registered approximate equality with 18.f4, or switched to a slow positional battle with an accumulation of small pluses, which was possible in the event of 18. ♘d3. The attempt to play more ambitiously leads to difficulties.

18...fxe4

19.♕b3?! And this is obviously in the wrong direction – see the previous note. 19.f4! exf3 20.♖xf3 ♖xf3 21.♘xf3 was essential, when although Black's position is already somewhat more pleasant, I do not think that White is in any serious danger of losing.

19...♗xe5 Quite a good 'structural' decision. The immediate 19...♕g5!? was also interesting, although in this case Black would have had to reckon with 20.♘xc6 ♗xc6 21.b5, when, if he does not find an immediate tactic on the kingside, his advantage can easily evaporate.

20.dxe5 ♕g5

21.♔h1 Another not very successful choice. The bishop exchange should have been opposed by 21.♕d1!, when it would be much more difficult for Black to develop his initiative. Levon was probably afraid of the knight manoeuvre 21...♘e7!?.

21...♗h5 Black's advantage has assumed visible proportions.

22.f3

One of the critical moments for me – not only in the game, but also in the tournament as a whole. After mak-

ing this move, Levon offered a draw. There was plenty to think about! Roughly one half of the thirty minutes that I had left on my clock were spent in doubts and hesitations. Of course, I should like to say that the decision, emotionally expressed at the press conference – 'if you don't continue in such a position, why play chess at all?' came to me easily and simply. In fact I was able to prefer the two birds in the bush to the one in the hand only after substantial internal effort. Of course, now, when I calmly look at the monitor, I am surprised – what was there to think about? It is not just that Black has an obvious advantage, but also that he is not in any danger. But during a game it is not often that one achieves the same clarity of thought and boldness, which one acquires in front of the screen of a powerful computer ☺, and in addition I have not yet gained the experience of successfully declining a draw in games with players such

as Aronian... I am pleased that I was able to dispel the mirages and overcome an important psychological barrier.

I should also like to dwell on another interesting factor. Levon could have offered a draw after playing 22.f4, which objectively was stronger and would have essentially reduced my choice to two sensible options: take the pawn *en passant* or conclude peace. However, apart from the psychological choice, Aronian also set me a chess choice! To a certain extent he took a risk, and the risk proved unjustified, but here it should be mentioned that the ability to offer a draw competently and at the right time has historically been an important instrument of warfare at the board. Thus in the given instance Levon disrupted the psychological background of a game that was going badly for him and obtained an additional chance, then he sharpened the play, and if I had not been fortunate enough to find a couple of strong replies with time-trouble approaching, the scenario could have changed, just as many historically important games and even whole tournaments have changed because of draw offers (after both refusals, and acceptances).

While not supporting a total rejection of the Sofia rules, I should mention that I have always been surprised by the absence of this argument in the stand of those who oppose them. At the board a player is very restricted in his choice of legal and legitimate means of conducting a psychological battle. So is it worth so categorically (and there are already calls to altogether forbid any conversations between players during a game!) removing one more of them, one which, besides, is by no means the least in importance?!

22...♕h6!

The time was spent not only on philosophical reasoning; I was also able to appreciate the strength of the subtle text-move, which emphasizes the restricted nature of White's position. I was less convinced by the simple

22...exf3 23.gxf3 ♕h4, although here also Black has an obvious advantage. **23.♖ce1 exf3 24.gxf3 ♖f7**

I think that this position already deserves a full ∓ assessment. It is hard to offer White any good advice, and so he decides on a desperate sharpening of the play.

25.♗c1 Objectively this merely hastens the end, but other continuations would have allowed Black to operate almost without any risk of going wrong. Now, however, the threat of e3-e4 at least somewhat unnerves him.

25...♗g6!? A solid and safe move, leading almost by force to a position that is practically lost for White, and in addition simplifying the play with time-trouble approaching.

Why then not simply an exclamation mark, you may ask? Because there was a possibility of playing even better! Here I missed an opportunity to decide the game quickly with a pretty combination: 25...♘xe5! 26.e4 ♗xf3+! (of course, not 26...♕f6? 27. exd5 exd5 28.♗b2, and White gains counterplay) 27.♖xf3 ♖xf3 28.♗xf3 ♕h3, and if 29.♗d1 there is 29...♘d3! 30.♔g1 ♖f8!,

ANALYSIS DIAGRAM

after which White has no defence! But seeing the possibility of such a 'quiet' strengthening of the position at the end of a variation is not at all easy. **26.e4 ♕h3 27.exd5 ♘d4 28.♕d1 ♘xe2 29.♕xe2 ♗h5**

White was practically forced to go in for this position, but it is completely dismal for him. None of the attempts to sacrifice the exchange is successful, and there only remains the continuation chosen by Aronian in the game. **30.♔g1 ♗xf3 31.♕f2**

31...♕g4+ Time-trouble was already making itself felt, and, failing to find a forced win, I decided on a simple and safe continuation. It is difficult to say which of the possible endgames is more advantageous for Black: that in the game, or the one reached after 31...♖af8!? 32.♕g3 ♕xg3+ 33.hxg3 ♗xd5 34.♖xf7 ♖xf7 35.♖f1! ♖c7 36.♗b2, when, strangely enough, it is not apparent how the immediate invasion of the black rook can be achieved. Apparently the preparatory doubling of the rooks was nevertheless rather more forceful, although the move in the game should not be condemned.

32.♕g3 ♕xg3+ 33.hxg3 ♗xd5 34.♗e3

Intending to prevent the imminent invasion by blocking the c-file.

34...a5!? I think that this is a good decision, although it would appear that a pawn exchange is not very advantageous to the stronger side. However, my reasoning was as follows: it is probable that the endgame is objectively won, and from the practical point of view it altogether does not seem possible to hold a position a pawn down, without counterplay and with a repulsive pawn structure. But at the same time, this is correct only if Black can quickly activate his rook and begin creating threats. Against this background, abstract considerations play a minor role.

35.b5

This desire not to open lines is logical. A sensible alternative was 35.♗d2 axb4 36.♗xb4 ♖c8 37.♖c1 ♖xf1+ 38.♖xf1 h6, but here, too, I think that Black should gradually achieve a decisive strengthening of his position.

35...a4 I decided that Black's position was strong enough not to have to calculate unnecessary variations after 35...♖xf1+! 36.♖xf1 ♗c4 37.♖d1 ♗xb5 38.♗b6. A questionable deci-

sion: here a second pawn is won, and the exchange of rooks, which possibly all the same does not lead to a draw, is easily avoided by, say, 38...♔f7. It is another matter that Black's winning chances are so great that he can also permit himself 'schematic' play.

36.♖xf7 ♔xf7 37.♖f1+ ♔g6 38. ♖f4 h6

39.♔f2 The best attempt to exploit the afore-mentioned schematic play was 39.♗b6!?, intending to set up a 'plug' with ♗c7 + b6. Black would not want to allow this, but in time-trouble it would be not at all easy to decide on the responsible move 39...♖c8!, involving the sacrifice of a pawn for the initiative, although after the possible 40.♖xa4 ♖c2 41.♖g4+ ♔h7 42.a4 g5 Black's winning chances are still considerable. In the game things were far easier for me.

39...♗b3!

Finally the black rook acquires its long-awaited freedom – its activation cannot be prevented. 'In passing' the time control is reached, and it becomes very difficult for White to hold the last lines of defence.

40.♖g4+ ♔h7 41.♖d4 ♖c8 42.b6 ♖c2+

43.♔e1?!

The final inaccuracy. True, there was also little joy for White after 43.♖d2 ♖c3 44.♗d4 ♖c1 – Black should gradually win. However, the move in the game leads to the immediate loss of another pawn.

43...♖a2 44.♗c1

44.♖d7 ♖xa3 45.♖xb7 ♗d5, and Black is winning.

44...♖g2

A simple pendulum manoeuvre leads to decisive gain of material.

45.♗f4 ♖g1+ 46.♔d2 ♖a1

My subsequent task was to cope with my nerves and the approaching second time-trouble. However, Black's position was so comfortably won, that it was not hard to do this. There followed:

47.♔c3 ♖xa3 48.♔b4 ♖a1 49. ♗d2 ♗d5 50.♔c3 ♖a2 51.♖d3 ♔g6 52.♖d4 a3 53.♖d3 ♔f5 54.♗d2 ♖a1 55.♔c3 ♖a2 56. ♗d2 ♔e4 57.♖e3+ ♔d4 58. ♗c1 ♖c2

And White resigned.

■ ■ ■

Altogether, Tomashevsky played 27 games in this Cup and was only eliminated in the semi-finals by Dmitry Andreikin, another gladiator that rose to new fame.

We cannot quite leave Morozevich yet, though. When I search for stories for my chess column, I usually begin by looking at the eccentric games of this unique player. And I am rarely disappointed. Morozevich was under pressure right from the start by a surprising loss to the much lower rated Bator Sambuev from Canada. He repaired that, however, by winning the next game and then doing the same in the first two playoff games.

His victory over Rafael Leitao in Round 2 wasn't fully convincing either. After having had a clearly winning position for a while, he suddenly gave the Brazilian a golden opportunity:

The conference room of the Scandic Hotel during one of the early rounds. In three weeks' time the World Cup shrank from a 128-player festival to a 4-game final match.

Morozevich-Leitao
Tromsø 2013 (2.1)
position after 34...♕e6

35.♕b4?? This is a much more advanced kind of mistake than what I did. Luckily for Morozevich, Leitao didn't notice 35...♘g3+ 36.hxg3 ♕h6+ 37.♔g1 ♗e3+ 38.♖f2 ♗xf2+ 39.♔xf2 ♕f6+ and picking up the rook on a1. 36.♔g1 ♗e3+ 37.♖f2 ♗xf2+ 38.♔xf2 ♕f6+ is about the same. Leitao chose **35...♗f6**, but then Morozevich showed his class and won in pretty style.

In Round 3 an interesting position occurred in the eighth match game between Morozevich and

Vitiugov – the first seven were drawn – with only five minutes and two-second increments.

Vitiugov-Morozevich
Tromsø 2013 (3.8)
position after 55...♖c2

How to draw this? That's not so easy with little time left unless you've studied basic endgame technique thoroughly. **56.♖c8?!** It's of course tempting to protect the pawn, but the thing here with doubled f-pawns, as commentators Susan Polgar and Lawrence Trent rightly pointed out, is that the extra pawn doesn't make a difference. With only one pawn on f4, I presume any grandmaster would instantly play 56.♖h3 and return with the rook the moment the pawn goes to f3. It doesn't matter actually that there is an extra pawn shielding checks from

behind. Black needs cover on the e- and g-files and that doesn't exist as he also needs his rook on the second rank to fend White's king off. After 56.♖h3 the position is a theoretical draw. **56...f3 57.c6?** Actually, White can still save the game by almost any other move, for instance 57.♔f1, 57.♖e8+, 57.♖a8. White just needs to realize that he shouldn't hang on to his c-pawn. **57...f2+ 0-1** There is no check from the side after 58.♔f1 ♔f3.

And that was the end of the adventure for Nikita Vitiugov. A shame actually, as it would have been great to see more fighting games with Vitiugov. What he did against Markus Ragger in Round 2 may be of theoretical importance.

GI 7.1 – D90
Evgeny Vitiugov
Markus Ragger
Tromsø 2013 (2.2)

1.d4 ♘f6 2.c4 g6 3.♘c3 d5 4.♘f3 ♗g7 5.h4!? This seems to be the latest hot shot against the Grünfeld. **5...dxc4** Magnus Carlsen survived with 5...c6 against Alexander Grischuk in the Candidates' tournament in London this year. Ragger's choice is much sharper. **6.e4 c5 7.d5 b5 8.h5** Who knows what the evaluation of this eventually will be. At this moment in history the combatants are pioneering the field. **8...0-0 9.hxg6 fxg6 10.e5 ♘g4 11.d6 e6**

12.♖xh7! It takes quite some guts, from both sides actually, just to get to such a position. It's all very messy. **12...♔xh7 13.♘g5+ ♔g8 14.♕xg4 ♖f5 15.♗e3 ♘c6 16.♕h4 ♘xe5 17.0-0-0 ♗d7 18.♘ce4**

18...♕a5? I won't even try to comment too much on a game like this, but this seems to be the crucial mistake. **19.♕h7+ ♔f8 20.♘xc5 ♖xg5** Eliminating some enemies, but not

enough. **21.♗xg5 ♕xa2 22.♖d4!** Even the rook enters the attack via f4. **22...♕a1+ 23.♔c2 ♘d3 24.♘xd7+ ♔f7 25.♘e5+!** Very cool! White is just one step ahead all the way. **25... ♘xe5 26.♖f4+ ♔e8 27.♕g8+ ♔d7 28.♕xg7+ ♔c6 29.♕xe5 ♕xf1 30.♕e4+ ♔b6 31.d7** Black resigned.

Some days later, Gata Kamsky needed a draw against Shakhriyar Mamedyarov – two more great fighters! – to advance, and that was the next duel in this line.

GI 7.1 – D90
Shakhriyar Mamedyarov
Gata Kamsky
Tromsø 2013 (4.2)

1.d4 ♘f6 2.c4 g6 3.♘c3 d5 4.♘f3 ♗g7 5.h4 dxc4 6.e4 0-0 Kamsky must have seen Vitiugov-Ragger and tries to improve with castling rather than 6...c5 and 7...b5. **7.h5 c5 8. hxg6 hxg6** Taking with the h-pawn is the difference from the previous game. **9.d5 b5 10.♗h6 ♗xh6 11. ♖xh6 b4 12.♘a4 ♔g7 13.♖h4 c3 14.bxc3 bxc3**

Somehow it looks as if White has won the theoretical battle. We need to see the rest of the game, as the way Kamsky secured the desired draw was simply amazing! **15.♖c1 ♖h8 16. ♖xh8 ♕xh8 17.♘xc5 ♘bd7 18. ♘xd7 ♗xd7 19.e5 ♘e4 20.♕d4 ♗f5 21.♕e3 ♕h1 22.♘d4 ♖b8 23.d6**

23...♖b2! We heard many players say that they had to play normal chess whenever they just needed a draw. I don't know what to call this, but to most other humans than Gata Kamsky and his likes, this is highly extraordinary play. **24.d7 ♖xf2 25.♕xf2 ♘xf2 26.♘xf5+ gxf5 27. d8♕ ♕h4!**

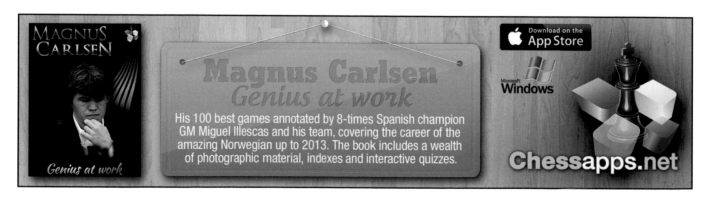

Incredibly, Black has enough counterplay for a draw here. Kamsky must have seen all this as early as move 23. Very impressive, indeed! **28.♔e2 ♛e4+ 29.♔xf2 ♛f4+ 30.♔e2 ♛xc1 31.♛d1 ♛b2+ 32.♔d3 ♛xa2** Black's strategy was simply to take some pawns! **33.♔xc3 ♛a5+ 34.♔b3** Draw. There are no winning chances for White after 34...♛xe5.

In the first game in this match Kamsky played what may have been the game of the tournament.

Gata Kamsky was a bit surprised by the praise that was showered on his attack against Shakhriyar Mamedyarov, as he felt he was almost forced to play brilliantly.

SI 40.1 – B47
Gata Kamsky
Shakhriyar Mamedyarov
Tromsø 2013 (4.1)

1.e4 c5 2.♘f3 e6 3.d4 cxd4 4. ♘xd4 ♘c6 5.♘c3 ♛c7 6.f4 d6 7.♗e3 ♘f6 8.♛f3 a6 9.♗d3 ♗e7 10.0-0 0-0 11.♔h1 ♗d7 12.♖ae1 b5 13.a3

13...♖ab8
It takes some deeper understanding to play this move. Pushing ...b5-b4 is of course in the air, preferably with ...a6-a5 included, but as it goes the focus soon is all on the centre and the kingside, and we see no Black activity on the queenside. **14.♘xc6 ♗xc6 15.♛h3**
Kamsky is following standard procedure. Black will soon have to do something to avoid being mated on h7.
15...♖fd8 16.♗d2 Putting the bishop on c1 seems like an option as the bishop is soon going to hang on d2.

However, Black can still play in the same way. One of many tricky lines is 16.♗c1 d5 17.e5 ♘e4 18.f5 (taking on e4 still doesn't work as the c2-pawn will fall in the end) 18...♛xe5! 19.fxe6 ♘f2+! 20.♖xf2 ♛xe1+ 21. ♖f1 ♛h4!, and Black is defending.
16...d5!?
At the last moment before e4-e5 was coming. 16...e5 was the alternative.
17.e5 17.exd5 exd5 will yield White nothing. **17...♘e4**

18.f5! Kamsky commented that he was surprised that everyone was so impressed by this game. He had no choice, he said, but to push forward. Still, the following attack is by no means obvious. **18...♘xd2 19.fxe6 ♘e4 20.exf7+ ♔h8**

21.♘xd5! Of course there is no way back now. **21...♗xd5 22.♖xe4 g6** 22...♗xe4 23.♗xe4 ♗h4 24.♛xh4 h6 25.e6 is unplayable for Black. **23. ♖ef4**

23...♔g7? This is the critical moment of the game. 24.♗xg6 has to be prevented and 23...♛c6 and 23...♛b6 are the alternatives. According to

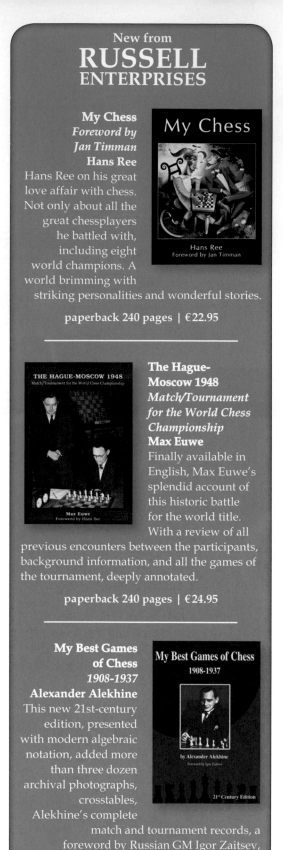
Kamsky, after 23...♕b6, he would have had to play 24.♕h6 (24.♖f6 ♗xf6 25.♖xf6 ♕d4! wins at once for Black) 24...♖f8 and then send another rook onto the fire with 25.♖f6!?. If we follow this line a few more moves – 25...♗xf6 26.♗xg6 (26.♖xf6 ♕d4 27. h3 ♖xf7) 26...♖xf7 27.♗xf7 ♗xf7 28. ♖xf6 ♕c7 – Black is probably better, but there still is a fight. After 23...♕c6 White can't leave g2 hanging, but now the rook sacrifice is an option. However, after 24.♖f6 ♗xf6 25.♖xf6 ♕b7, 26.♗xg6? doesn't work due to 26... ♗xg2+. White would have had to continue with 26.e6 in this line and it's still messy. **24.e6 ♖f8 25.♕e3** Now comes some very nasty queen manoeuvring. **25...♗c5** Black has to avoid a diagonal check at all cost. **26.♕e1 ♗d6 27.♖h4 ♗e7**

28.♕e3! There are actually two black diagonals that Black has to cover, and that is one too many. **28...h5** 28... ♗xh4 29.♕d4+ ♔h6 30.♕xh4+ ♔g7 31.♕f6+ ♔h6 32.♖f4! was Black's problem. **29.♕d4+ ♔h6 30.♖xh5+** Black resigned. 30...gxh5 31.♖f6+ is mate, and 30...♔xh5 31.♕xd5+ ♔h6 32.♕e4 is also hopeless.

Anton Korobov was among the last eight players remaining. The Ukrainian impressed by almost beating Vladimir Kramnik in the second game in the quarter finals. That was the only game in which Kramnik was in trouble. But Kramnik survived, and, as he had won the first game, that was it for Korobov.

Still, Korobov made many fans, not only by his play but also by his orig-inal and philosophical post-game comments. Korobov has a very high rating and is only 28 years old, but he has never played for the Ukrainian national team. It shone through that there is a story here and that being a chess player in Ukraine is not always a bed of roses.

Beating Hikaru Nakamura in an event like this is also quite an achievement. We follow the end of the crucial second game.

Korobov-Nakamura
Tromsø 2013 (4.2)
position after 34.h5

34...♖h8 Nakamura covers the h-file, but he misses the neighbouring file. **35.♔c2 ♔g8 36.♖hg1!** Black loses control of everything. **36...♔g7 37.hxg6 hxg6 38.♘xg6 ♖xe1 39. ♖xe1 ♖h7 40.♘e7+ ♔f7**

41.d5! It wasn't hard to tell which way the wind was blowing by Nakamura's body language. After 41.♘xf5 ♗f8 the American could still fight on. **41...cxd5 42.c6 ♗a8 43.c7 ♗b7 44.c8♕ ♗xc8 45.♘xc8 ♖h6 46.♘e7 ♖h2 47.b4** Black resigned. There are no tricks, not even for Hikaru Nakamura.

It's always interesting to listen to Garry Kasparov. During the final, when not so much was happening on the board as there was only one game to follow, Dirk Jan ten Geuzendam and Nigel Short, the commentators for the last rounds, managed to get hold of the very busy man on Skype for a whole hour. When Magnus was a young teenager, Kasparov wasn't quite approving of his sauntering approach, but with a talent like Magnus's perhaps anything would do. Daniil Dubov (17), Russia, and Wei Yi (14), China's latest wonderboy, both impressed by winning their first two matches, but Kasparov thought otherwise. He could see no future world champion potential in those between 15 and 20 today. Wei Yi is slightly outside that range, though, so perhaps there is hope for him! No matter what, knocking out Alexey Shirov in Round 2 was quite an achievement.

Fourteen-year-old Wei Yi was perhaps the biggest sensation in Tromsø. The young Chinese GM reached Round 4 and particularly impressed with his dashing win against Alexey Shirov.

NOTES BY
Wei Yi

SI 23.1 – B84
Wei Yi
Alexey Shirov
Tromsø 2013 (2.2)

It's the second round. My opponent is Alexey Shirov from Latvia. I've read his famous book *Fire on Board*! It contains beautiful games and I was really impressed by his attacking skills, the tactics and the sacrifices! I made a draw with black in the first game and now I want to fight for a win.
1.e4 c5 2.♘f3 d6 3.d4 cxd4 4. ♘xd4 ♘f6 5.♘c3 a6 6.♗e3 e6
I had prepared for this because he plays the Scheveningen frequently.
7.♗e2 ♕c7 8.♕d2 b5 9.f3
A rare line. Compared to 9.a3, it prevents the ...♗b7-♘c6 plan. Now 9... ♗b7 will be met by 10.a4!. My opponent has played this line from both sides, so I suppose he's very familiar with it. But I wanted to challenge him.

9...♘bd7
As said, 9...♗b7 is not a good choice because of 10.a4 b4 11.♘a2 d5 12.e5!.

ANALYSIS DIAGRAM

and now if Black goes 12...♕xe5, play continues 13.♗f4 ♕h5 14.g4 ♕g6 15.♗d3 ♘e4 16.fxe4 dxe4 17.♗c4 e3 18.♗xe3 ♗xh1 19.0-0-0, and White is winning.

12...♘fd7 is the only move, when after 13.f4 ♘c5 14.0-0 ♘e4 15.♕e1 White has a pleasant position.

Instead of the text-move, 9...b4 was played in the game Inarkiev-Le Quang Liem, Khanty-Mansiysk FIDE World Rapid 2013. After 10.♘a4 ♘bd7 11.c3 bxc3 12.♘xc3 ♗b7 I think it's better to play 13.♖c1 (in the game White played 13.0-0) 13...♖c8 (or 13...♕b8 14.♗d1!) 14.0-0 ♕b8 15.♘b3!, with the idea of 16.♘a5.

Finally, 9...♗e7 deserves attention: 10.a4 (10.g4 0-0) 10...b4 11.♘a2 e5 12.♘f5 ♗xf5 13.exf5 ♘c6 14.♘xb4 ♘xb4 15.♕xb4 ♕d7, with a complex position.
10.a3

10...h5 After 10...♖b8 White can play 11.0-0 or 11.0-0-0. There are

also some games by strong players in the variation 10...♗b7 11.0-0-0 d5 12.exd5 ♘xd5 13.♘xd5 ♗xd5, when White has three continuations: 14.♖he1, 14.♔b1 and 14.♗f4.

In case of 10...♗e7 White can play 11.0-0-0 (or 11.g4) 11...0-0 12.g4 ♘b6 13.g5 ♘fd7 14.f4 ♖e8 15.h4 threatening 16.g6. This is very dangerous for Black.

Another continuation that has been seen is 10...♘e5 11.0-0-0 ♗e7, which occurred in the game Inarkiev-Shomoev, Ekaterinburg 2013. I think that after 12.g4 the position is unclear, for example: 12...♘fd7 13.♗g5! ♗xg5 14.♕xg5 0-0 15.f4 ♘c4 16.♘d5 ♕b7 17.♘e7+ ♔h8 18.♘ef5 exf5 19.♘xf5 g6 20.♗xc4 bxc4 21.♘xd6.

11.0-0-0 My opponent played 11.0-0 to beat Van Wely back in 1995. After that Black can choose between 11...♗b7 and 11...♗e7.

11...♖b8 12.♗xb5

Only this way. After 12.♘dxb5 axb5 13.♘xb5 ♖xb5 14.♗xb5 ♗e7 Black has a promising position.

12...axb5 13.♘dxb5 ♕b7 14.♕xd6

14...♗xd6 I don't think this is good. The resulting endgame is easy to play for White. At the 2005 Canadian Open my opponent played 14...♗e7 against Bologan, when White can continue 15.a4 (that game went 15.♗f4 e5! 16.♗xe5 ♕xb5! 17.♘xb5 ♖xb5, and Black had a good game due to 18.♕c6 ♖c5!; 15.♕c7?! is not good in view of 15...0-0) 15...h4 16.♕c7 ♕xc7 17.♘xc7+ ♔f8 18.♘3b5 h3 (this is the point of 15...h4!) 19.g3 ♘e5 20.♖hf1 ♘e8, and Black has no problems.

During my preparation, I had mainly looked at other lines after 9.f3, because I didn't think he would repeat what he had played before.

15.♘xd6+ ♔e7 16.♘xb7 ♗xb7 17.♖d4 ♖hd8

Maybe he should put his rooks on c8 and a8 to keep my pawns in check: 17...♖a8 18.♖hd1 ♖hc8 19.a4 ♗a6.

18.♖hd1 ♘e5 19.a4

Another idea was 19.♖xd8 ♖xd8 20.♗c5+ ♔e8 21.a4.

I also considered 19.♘b5 during the game, but was afraid of 19...♖xd4 20.♗xd4 (in fact, I can play 20.♘xd4, and I'm better) 20...♘fd7 21.a4 ♗c6.

19...♖xd4 20.♗xd4 ♘fd7 21.b3

After 21.b4 ♘c4! 22.♔b1 g5 23.♔a2 ♗a8 24.b5 g4 Black has counterplay on the kingside.

21...g5 22.♘b5

22...g4? Too hasty. Maybe Black had overlooked White's reply. He should have driven away White's knight first: 22...♗c6 23.♘a7 ♗b7.

23.♗b2 Now it's too late.

23...gxf3 24.♗a3+

24...♔f6?!

Black misses his best chance for counterplay.

After 24...♔d8! 25.♗d6 ♖a8 26.♗xe5 fxg2 27.♗f6+ ♔e8 the position is unclear, e.g., after 28.♘c7+? ♔f8 29.♘xa8 ♘xf6 30.♖g1 ♗xe4 31.♘b6 h4 White is in danger. But White can play 28.♘d6+ ♔f8 29.♗g5 ♗a6 30.c4!, when Black's bishop is out of the game and White has the advantage.

25.gxf3 ♔g5 26.♘d4 ♗a6

After 26...♔f4 White keeps his advantage with 27.♔b1 ♔e3 28.♗c1+ ♔f2 29.♗f4.

27.♔b1 ♖b7 28.♖g1+ ♔f6

29.♗b2?!

Not the best. Clearly stronger was 29.f4 ♘g6 30.e5+ ♔g7 31.♖g5.

29...♔e7 Better was 29...♘g6.

30.♖g5 h4 31.f4 ♘g6 32.♘xe6

Also strong was 32.f5 exf5 33.exf5 ♘ge5 34.♖h5.

32...fxe6 33.♖xg6 ♘c5

Better was 33...♘b4, when after 34.♗a3 ♘f7 35.♗xb4 (better is 35.♖xe6 ♖xb3+ 36.cxb3 ♔xe6) 35...♔xg6 the win is not so clear.

34.f5 ♔f7 35.♖f6+ ♔e7 36.♖h6 ♔f7 37.♖xh4 exf5 38.exf5 ♖d7 39.♗d4

39.♗a3 ♖d5 40.♖h7+ ♔g8 41.♖c7 would also have done the job.

39...♖d5

40.♖f4 Also winning was 40.♗xc5 ♖xc5 41.b4 ♖xf5 42.c4, and the pawns are too strong.
40...♗c8 41.♗xc5
This transposes to an easily won endgame.
41...♖xc5 42.♔b2 ♔f6 43.b4 ♖c7 44.♔b3 ♗xf5 45.c3 ♖h7
After 45...♔e5 White simply plays 46.♖h4.
46.b5 ♔e5 47.♖d4 ♖xh2 48. a5 ♗h3 49.a6 ♗f1 50.a7 ♖h8 51.♔b4 ♗g2 52.♖d2 ♗f3 53.♔a5 ♖c8
53...♗d5 will not stop the pawns either: 54.c4 ♗xc4 55.b6.
54.♖d3

54...♗g2
After 54...♗d5 White can even sacrifice his rook: 55.♔a6 ♗g2 56.b6 ♗f1 57.b7 ♗xd3+ 58.♔b6, and wins.
55.♔a6 ♖f8 56.♖d2 ♗a8 57.c4 ♖c8 58.c5

Now after 58...♖xc5 59.♖d8 ♗f3 60. a8♕ ♗xa8 61.♖xa8 White has a winning rook ending. Black resigned. This win allowed me to progress to the third round!

■ ■ ■

Perhaps we have to search in the 1990-generation to find Magnus Carlsen's next contenders? In Tromsø, Ian Nepomniachtchi, who actually used to finish ahead of Magnus in youth championships some 10 years ago, lost to Wei Yi as early as Round 1. Sergey Karjakin, whose talent and potential was, of course, established long ago, was defeated by Andreikin in Round 4. The two 1990'ers that did best this time were Maxime Vachier-Lagrave and Dmitry Andreikin.

The French star seems to have added an extra dimension to his play lately. His score in this Cup was very convincing. He started by winning the first five games, and proceeded as far as Round 4 without spending too much energy. Against the Cuban Isam Reynaldo Ortiz in Round 2, however, it must be mentioned that Vachier-Lagrave was in dire straits:

Ortiz-Vachier-Lagrave
Tromsø 2013 (2.1)
position after 42...e3

The pawns are under control after either 43.gxf4 or 43.g4. Instead, Ortiz gave his opponent a golden opportunity. **43.♔e2?? g4!** Now suddenly the pawns are rolling in. **44.♖f7 gxf3+ 45.♔e1 ♞e5 46.♖xf4 ♖c6** It's even a mating attack. **47.♔d1 e2+ 48.♔d2 ♖c1** White resigned.

Suarez surprised by beating Judit Polgar in the first round, but missed his chance here. In the next round another Cuban, Leinier Dominguez, had to bite the dust against the same French tornado.

NOTES BY
Maxime Vachier-Lagrave

SI 4.1 – B94
**Maxime Vachier-Lagrave
Leinier Dominguez**
Tromsø 2013 (3.1)

1.e4 c5 2.♘f3 d6 3.d4 cxd4 4. ♘xd4 ♘f6 5.♘c3 a6 6.♗g5

Most of my preparation for the World Cup was aimed at my black openings, the Slav and the Caro-Kann, which meant that I had to be clever with white and try to surprise my opponents. I had almost never played the critical 6.♗g5 against the Najdorf, but from time to time I had spent a couple of days checking this position from the black side, which meant that my workload during the free day, although considerable, was manageable.
6...♘bd7 7.♗c4 ♕b6 8.♗b3 e6 9.♕d2 ♗e7 10.0-0-0 ♘c5 11. ♖he1 ♕c7 12.♔b1

12...h6
After 12...0-0, 13.f4 h6 14.h4! is very good for White, as Rublevsky has

shown in recent years, for instance transposing via the Sozin Variation, 6.♗c4, against me in Warsaw most recently: 14...b5 15.e5 dxe5 16.fxe5 ♘h7 (16...♘g4 17.♕f4! gives White a dangerous attack) 17.♗xe7 ♕xe7

ANALYSIS DIAGRAM

18.♘e4! (this yields White a clear advantage) 18...♗b7 19.♘xc5 ♕xc5 20.g4 ♕e7 21.♕h2 ♖fd8 22.g5 hxg5 23.hxg5 ♕xg5 24.♖g1 ♕e3 25.c3 ♗e4+ 26.♔a1 ♗g6 27.♖xg6 fxg6 28. ♗xe6+ ♔h8 29.♖h1 ♕h6 30.♕g2 1-0, Rublevsky-Vachier-Lagrave, Warsaw rapid 2012.

13.♗h4 b5

This is premature, but I spent a lot of time here, as I couldn't remember the useful content of my work the day before.

Instead of this move I had mainly focused on 13...0-0 14.♗g3 b5 (14... ♘h5?! runs into 15.♘f5! ♘xg3 – bad is 15...exf5? 16.♘d5 ♕d8 17.♘xe7+ ♕xe7 18.♗xd6 ♘xb3 19.axb3 ♕d8 20.♗xf8 ♕xf8 21.♕a5 – 16.♘xe7+ ♕xe7 17.hxg3, and White has a pleasant advantage) 15.e5 dxe5 16.♗xe5 ♕b6, with a double-edged position.

14.♗d5?!

Maxime Vachier-Lagrave was in great shape. The Frenchman won his first five games, picked up 23 rating points and reached the semi-finals, where it took Vladimir Kramnik to knock him out.

Not the best. Stronger was 14.♗xf6! ♗xf6 15.♘f5 (a typical manoeuvre that works well here) 15...exf5 (also interesting is 15...♗b7!? 16.♘xd6+ ♕xd6 – 16...♘xd6 is met strongly by 17.e5! – 17.♕xd6 ♘xd6 18.e5! – otherwise Black has definite compensation for the pawn, so White is well advised to open the e-file and get play for all his pieces, especially the bishop on b3 – 18...♗h4 19.exd6 ♗xf2 20. ♖e2, with a white edge) 16.♘d5 ♕d8 17.♘xf6+ ♕xf6

ANALYSIS DIAGRAM

18.e5! (the critical move that I failed to remember from my preparation) 18...dxe5 (on 18...♕d8 White has 19.exd6+ ♘e6 20.♗xe6! ♗xe6 21. d7+ ♔e7 22.g4!, weakening Black's

king even more: 22...fxg4 23.♕b4+ ♔f6 24.♖d6, with a relentless attack) 19.♖xe5+ ♗e6 (19...♘e6? loses to 20.♕d6) 20.♖xc5, with a slight but definite edge.

14...♗b7?!

This is a mistake. Leinier probably hadn't overlooked the strong white follow-up, as it is typical, but I suppose he thought that with so many exchanges it couldn't work so well for White.

I thought that 14...♖b8 was by far the best move for Black, after which I probably would have gone for 15. ♗c6+ ♗d7 (after 15...♔f8?!, 16.a3 is the quiet option when 16...b4? 17.axb4 ♖xb4 18.♗xf6 ♗xf6 19.♘d5 gives White a big advantage) 16.♗xd7+

ANALYSIS DIAGRAM

16...♘cxd7! (16...♕xd7 17.♘b3 ♘xb3 18.axb3 gives White the initiative, as he is safe, while Black has to lose time to protect the d6-pawn with 18...♖d8, when White continues 19.f4) 17.f4 b4 18.♘a4 0-0 (18...♘xe4?? is a blunder because of 19.♖xe4 ♗xh4 20.♘f5), with unclear play.

15.♗xb7 ♕xb7

In case of 15...♘xb7 16.f4 0-0 (16...♘xe4?! loses to 17.♖xe4 ♗xh4 18.♘d5) 17.e5 White is clearly better

after 17...♘e4 (the only move) 18.♖xe4 ♗xh4 19.♘f3 ♗e7 20.f5! exf5 21.♘d5.

16.♗xf6! gxf6 16...♗xf6 runs into 17.♘f5!, when after 17...exf5 18.exf5+ ♔f8 19.♕xd6+ ♗e7 20.♕e5 ♖e8 21.♘d5 ♘d7 22.♕e4 Black has no good defence. Looking at the position at this point, it is quite obvious that Black cannot afford to play this way, but a few moves back it was much harder to imagine that, despite the low number of minor pieces, White's attack could take on such gigantic proportions.

17.♕e3

Now it is clear that I am far better, as Black has a lot of weaknesses and very little counterplay. But I still have to play precisely in the next few moves to prevent Black from regrouping.

17...0-0-0

18.♘b3

It goes without saying that I considered 18.♘d5, the move that the computer likes, but what I missed was that after 18...exd5 19.exd5 ♖d7 20.♘c6 ♗d8 (20...♖e8 21.♕xh6 is excel-

lent for White) 21.♕g3! the sudden 22.♕g7, trapping Black's rook, is a very serious threat. Still, in a practical game it makes sense to gradually improve your position instead of immediately throwing in pieces at the risk of giving Black counterplay.

18...♘d7

18...♘xb3 19.axb3 ♔b8 20.f4 leads to a textbook advantage for White. Yet it may have been objectively best in view of White's strong reply in the game.

19.a4!

I am not a big fan of committal moves when they are not needed in a clearly better position, but I wanted to avoid the annoying possibility of ...♘e5-c4, and I finally came to the conclusion that I ran much less risk by opening the queenside.

19...b4 20.♘a2 ♘e5

21.♕e2!

Now Black's knight is repelled and I get the chance to attack all Black's weaknesses: a6, b4, e6 and f7 are potentially in trouble!

21...♖d7

White is clearly better after 21...♔b8 22.f4 ♘c6 23.♕h5! ♖hf8 24.♖e2.

22.f4 ♘c6

23.f5! Again the right decision, though an easy one. Black's position is on the verge of falling apart.

23...exf5 24.♘d4 I had missed the regrouping 24.exf5 d5 25.♘ac1, using the now weak c5-square, when apparently Black's position is pretty hopeless. At the same time I like the text-move, which makes good use of all Black's weaknesses.

24...♘xd4 25.♖xd4 a5 26.♖d5

26...♗d8 After 26...fxe4 White has the cute zwischenzug 27.♕c4+!, which I hadn't really considered prior to taking on e4, but after 27...♖c7 28.♕xe4 Black can no longer defend the pawn on a5, and White also gets the possibility of checking on f5 first. The position is hopeless for Black.

27.♖xf5 ♖e8 28.♖b5 ♕c6

29.♘c1! Now that my knight is joining the fray, Black's weaknesses will probably be too numerous to handle.

29...♖e5

After 29...♖de7 30.♕f3 (30.♕g4+ ♕d7 31.♕f3, with an undeniable advantage, was my intention) 30...♖xe4 31.♖d1 ♖c4 White has

ANALYSIS DIAGRAM

32.♖d4!. I will not pretend that I saw this move, but it is clear that the tactics are very likely to favour White in such a nice positional situation: 32...♖e4 (32...♖xc2 fails to 33.♕f5+) 33.♕f5+ ♔c7 34.♖xc4 ♖xc4 35.♖xa5,

ANALYSIS DIAGRAM

and White should be winning.

30.♘b3 ♖xb5 31.axb5 ♕b6 32. ♖d1!

And the knight arrives with decisive effect indeed.

32...a4 33.♘d4 ♛c5 34.♘c6 ♗b6 35.♖d4 b3 36.cxb3 axb3 37.♖c4 ♛g1+ 38.♖c1 ♛e3 39.♘d4+ ♛xc1+ 40.♔xc1 ♗xd4

The smoke has cleared and Black does not even come close to managing any kind of blockade here.

41.♛d3 ♗e5

42.h4

A potential passed h-pawn is an asset that in most circumstances should be clung to.

42...♖c7+ 43.♔d1 ♗xb2

Or 43...♖c2 44.♛xb3 ♖xb2 45.♛xf7 ♖xb5 46.♛e8+ and wins.

44.♛xb3 ♗e5

44...♗d4 loses to 45.♛d5 ♗c5 46.♛a8+ ♔d7 47.♛f8.

45.♛d5!

Now Black fails to blockade the b-pawn with the king, and after:

45...♔b8 46.b6 ♖e7 47.g4 ♗g3 48.♛c6

he has no move against the king's journey to a6, followed by b7 and mate.

48...f5 49.exf5 ♗xh4 50.f6!

Black resigned.

■ ■ ■

Vachier-Lagrave also beat Boris Gelfand and Fabiano Caruana, but eventually had to bow to Vladimir Kramnik in Round 6, which was the semi-final. Maxime Vachier-Lagrave is now number 15 in the world and to me it seems that there is potential for more.

Finally, only two players were left in the big playing hall. Dmitry Andreikin said he was horribly badly prepared for the tournament and laughed at his wins with the Torre Attack against both Peter Svidler and Sergey Karjakin. For a moment I was led to believe that Andreikin was another of those fighters without a proper opening repertoire, but his win against the Vietnamese Nguyen Ngoc Truong Son – another great player born in 1990! – in Round 2 suggests otherwise.

NOTES BY
Dmitry Andreikin

CA 3.1 – E04
Dmitry Andreikin
Nguyen Ngoc Truong Son
Tromsø 2013 (2.2)

1.d4 d5 2.♘f3 ♘f6 3.c4 e6 4.g3 dxc4 5.♗g2 ♘c6 6.0-0 ♖b8

This line has a dubious reputation and statistics for Black to go with it. The move ...a7-a6 is safer and more popular. My opponent definitely relied on the element of surprise. And not in vain.

7.♘c3 I spent a lot of time on this logical move. The other line White can go for is 7.♗g5!?.

7...b5
Forced activity. Otherwise, after having taken the pawn on c4 back, White would gain an advantage in the centre.

8.♘e5
Such moves are made automatically. Of course, the opening of the diagonal and the d-file favours White.

8...♘xe5 9.dxe5 ♘d7
Up to this point my opponent had played quickly. As for me, I had lots of options. I made an interesting choice.

10.♛d4!? This move is not a novelty, but it doesn't look obvious, so my opponent hadn't considered it during his preparation for the game. The idea is that if the black knight moves, the white queen moves to g4, threatening Black's kingside.

10.♗c6 used to be the fashion, but I was sure my opponent was ready for this. An excellent game with that move was played by Gleizerov in 2000: 10.♗c6 a6 11.♛d4 ♗b7 12. ♗xb7 ♖xb7 13.♖d1 ♗e7 14.♛g4 g6 15.♗h6 ♛c8 16.♛f4 ♘b6 17.♗g7 ♖g8 18.♛h6 ♘d5 19.♘xd5 exd5 20. ♖xd5 c6 21.♖d2 ♖d7 22.♖ad1 ♖xd2 23.♖xd2 ♗f8 24.♗xf8 ♖xf8 25.♛h4 c5 26.♖d6 a5 27.♛f6 a4 28.e6 ♛c7 29.♖d7 1-0, Gleizerov-Malakhatko, Bydgoszcz 2000.

10...b4?! My plan was a success! This move was made after a long think.
Of course, 10...♗c5 11.♛g4 ♔f8 12.♛h5, with an attack, looks dangerous for Black.
The computer recommends 10...c5!? 11.♛f4 ♛c7 12.a4 bxa4!.

With cool and collected play Dmitry Andreikin reached the final. In the classical games he spilled some rating points, but his merciless determination in the tiebreaks made him the revelation of the World Cup.

11.♘a4!? The well-known theoretician E. Postny prefers to move the knight back to the centre, 11.♘e4, but it didn't yield him much after 11...♘b6 12.♕xd8+ ♔xd8 13.♗e3 ♗b7 14.♖ac1 ♗e7 15.♘d2 ♗d5 16.♖fd1 ♔c8 17.♗xb6 axb6 18.♘xc4 ♗xg2 19.♔xg2 ♖d8 20.♖xd8+ ♔xd8 21.b3 ♖a8 22.♖c2 b5 23.♘d2 c5, and the game Postny-Aleksandrov, Wroclaw 2009, ended in a draw after 35 moves.

11...♘b6 It's difficult to condemn this move, because Black's position is already dangerous. K. Landa tried to play more fundamentally with 11...c5, but his idea was also a failure, as he lost to M. Krylov with it in 2010. **12.♕xd8+**

It's rare that a queen swap is useful for the attacker. Now White develops a promising initiative.
12...♔xd8 13.♖d1+

13...♔e8?!
There is no good way out of the check. After 13...♘d7, 14.♗c6! is very good for White. And White is also on top after 13...♘d5 14.e4 ♗d7 15.exd5 ♗xa4 16.♖d4, or 13...♗d7 14.♘xb6 ♖xb6 15.♗e3 c5 16.♖ac1.
The most tenacious defence involved moving the king to another square: 13...♔e7!? 14.♘xb6 axb6 15.♗c6! f6 16.♗f4 ♔f7 (and not 16...f5 17.♗g5+ ♔f7 18.♗d8!) 17.exf6 e5 18.♗xe5 ♗e6, although here, too, White clearly has good chances.

14.♘xb6 This cements White's advantage.

14...♖xb6 The computer insists on taking back with the a-pawn, but this would look strange after the previous move, as it would allow White a useful check on c6. **15.♗e3**

Having made this move, I was sure I'd win. Black loses the battle on the queenside.
15...c5 16.a3 White should play in the correct order. **16...b3 17.♖ac1 ♗a6** Black has no choice, he has to defend. Strangely enough, my opponent was still in a good mood.
18.a4!

The winning move. The rooks and bishops cannot break down Black's

ANASTASIYA KARLOVICH

defences, but the pawn lends a helping hand.

18...♗b7 Black has to admit to the failure of his strategy.

White also wins after 18...f6 19.a5 ♖b8 20.♗c6+ ♔f7 21.♖d7+ ♔g6 22.♖xa7.

19.♖xc4 ♗xg2 20.♔xg2 ♖c6 21.♖d3

Black is in great trouble. His bishop and rook on the kingside never entered the game. Now the time had come for me to harvest pawns. There is no need for any further comment. It was easy to convert the position into a victory.

21...f6 22.exf6 gxf6 23.♖xb3 ♖b6 24.♖b5 ♔f7

25.♗xc5 ♖xb5 26.axb5 ♗xc5 27.♖xc5 ♖d8 28.♖c7+ ♔g6 29.♖xa7 ♖d2 30.b4 ♖d4 31.b6 ♖xb4 32.♖b7 e5 33.♖b8 ♔g7 34.b7 ♖b3 35.e4 ♖b2 36.♔f3 ♖b3+ 37.♔g4

The white king can safely walk over to the queenside, which the black king cannot, as 37...♔f7 allows the deadly 38.♖h8. Black resigned.

■ ■ ■

The highly deserving winner of the whole World Cup was Vladimir Kramnik. He was perhaps in danger in the second quarter final game against Anton Korobov, but he had won the first game in that match, so compared to what adventures the other players had to go through this was just a tiny detail. Kramnik's win seemed very convincing, with rock-solid play throughout. It was interesting to hear how even Kasparov showed his respect for his previous rival. Kramnik prevents dangers even before his opponents realize there may be something, Kasparov said, to which commentator Nigel Short quipped that his strategy against Kasparov in 1993 had been just that: to attack fiercely to let Kasparov spend his time finding out if there actually was something real about it.

Kramnik gave Andreikin no chances after winning the first final game:

NOTES BY
Vladimir Kramnik

QO 7.1 – D58
Vladimir Kramnik
Dmitry Andreikin
Tromsø 2013 (7.1)

1.d4 e6 2.c4 ♘f6

I noticed that Dmitry often begins with this move order, via 1...e6. This is quite original, since the only plus is that Black does not allow 2.♗g5, which he himself employs with white. But in general this continuation is not dangerous, whereas White has quite a good alternative – 2.e4!. Nevertheless he stubbornly sticks to this move order.

3.♘f3 d5 4.♗g5 ♗e7 5.♘c3 h6 6.♗h4 0-0 7.e3 I did not rule out the fact that in our match there would be four Queen's Gambits, like Capablanca with Alekhine; it is possible to play one and the same position with different colours. Dmitry thought for quite a long time and chose:

7...b6

I gained the feeling that his knowledge here was, to put it mildly, superficial. Possibly he had prepared 7...♘e4, but he decided against playing this, considering me to be an expert in this field.

8.♗d3 One of the main systems.

8...dxc4

Again after prolonged thought. However, this is an inaccurate move order. Usually Black plays 8...♗b7 9.0-0 ♘bd7, and only after a move such as 10.♗g3 does he exchange on c4. And if 10.♕e2 there follows 10...c5, with a more favourable version for Black. He probably wanted to avoid variations with the exchanges on f6 and d5, although theory does not consider them dangerous. The immediate 8...dxc4 allows White additional possibilities.

9.♗xc4 ♗b7 10.0-0 ♘bd7 11.♕e2

This position is assessed as better for White; his advantage is slight, but stable. However, the Queen's Gambit is such a solid opening, that even if you do not play it altogether accurately things do not turn out very badly.

11...a6

By this point my opponent had spent at least half a hour, and possibly even forty minutes. Here 11...♘e4 is normally played, but White gains a comfortable plus by 12.♘xe4 ♗xe4 (or 12...♗xh4 13.♘c3) 13.♗g3.

11...♘d5 is interesting – at least, if Black chooses this plan, it is probably better to play this immediately, without a7-a6. Possibly Dmitry did not like 12.♘xd5 exd5 13.♗xe7 ♕xe7 14.♗a6, but this would not appear to give anything special after 14...♗xa6 15.♕xa6 c5.

12.♖fd1

Played with infinite wisdom (for the moment, White tries to refrain from a4), although I am not sure that in the end this is the most sensible move.

Of course, in the first instance I considered the most logical reply 12.a4, but then 12...♘e4 gains in strength (if 12...♘d5 13.♗xd5 exd5 14.♗xe7 ♕xe7 White has the important resource 15.a5, guaranteeing him a pleasant positional advantage: the pawn structure is fixed, Black is deprived of the possibility of playing ...c7-c5, and this means that he is obliged to play not with hanging pawns, but with an isolani, which with such a light-squared bishop is not very pleasant): 13.♘xe4 ♗xh4 14.♘c3 ♗e7 15.♖fd1 c6 – here the inclusion of ...a6/a4 is in Black's favour, and he has an acceptable position, although White retains some advantage.

After the move in the game it seemed to me that 12...b5 13.♗d3

ANALYSIS DIAGRAM

was dangerous for Black – White wants to play a2-a4, and 13...c5 is not possible because of 14.dxc5. 13...♖c8 14.a4 b4 15.♘b1 a5 16.♘bd2 c5 17.♗b5 is also bad for Black. However, the computer makes the strange move 13...♕e8 and does not see any particular grounds for concern. If 14.e4 Black is able to reply 14...c5, while in the event of 14.a4 b4 15.♘b1 c5 16.♘bd2 White has structurally a very pleasant position, but this does not impress the 'wizard': it continues 16...cxd4 17.♘xd4 ♘c5 and thinks that Black is close to equality. Well, perhaps this is so, I will not argue.

12...♘d5 Also quite a good move.

Here I don't in fact like Houdini's first line: it suggests 13.♘xd5 exd5 14.♗xe7 ♕xe7 and now 15.♗d3 or 15.♗b3, but it seems to me that after this Black gets in ...c7-c5 and he has no serious problems. Although White retains slight pressure thanks to the fact that the bishop is on b7, and not on e6, I was not very satisfied with this.

I realized that I should probably go in for 13.♗xd5 exd5 14.♗xe7 ♕xe7 15.a3. White again does not allow the creation of hanging pawns: ...c7-c5 is not possible on account of dxc5, while if 15...♘f6 there follows 16.b4.

And yet I took a decision based on my opponent's style: Dmitry is a very solid player, he defends well in passive positions of this sort, and therefore I preferred more dynamic play.

13.♗g3

Perhaps objectively this is not the strongest continuation, but here more complicated positions arise. Against another opponent I would possibly have chosen 13.♗xd5.

13...♘xc3 14.bxc3

14...♗d6

14...♘f6 would seem to be logical, but here White has a very pleasant game after 15.♗d3 (with the intention of e3-e4) 15...♘e4 16.♕c2 ♘xg3 17.hxg3. White wants to exchange bishops by the manoeuvre ♗h7-e4, which secures him an enduring advantage. The exchange on f3 does not improve the situation – this position with opposite-coloured bishops is very unpleasant for Black. And if he forestalls White's idea with 17...♕d5, then after, say, 18.a4 the position of the pawn on a6 tells – if it were on its initial square, White would have only a nominal advantage, whereas here in the event of ...c7-c5 the b6-pawn will always be weak. I think that Black played more accurately.

15.e4

Here I was over-hasty, intending to achieve a position which it would have been better to obtain via a different move order.

Stronger was 15.a4 ♗xg3 16.hxg3 c5 (I thought that 16...♘f6 would stop e3-e4, but in fact after 17.♗d3 I will advance the e-pawn sooner or later) 17.e4. It was this position that I was intending to play; in my opinion it is quite pleasant for White, once again thanks to the fact that the moves ...a6, a4 have been included – the b6-pawn will soon come under fire by the rook on b1, and in addition the rook on a8 cannot tear itself away from the a6-pawn.

15...♗xg3 16.hxg3 b5!

I underestimated this resource.

17.♗d3

17...♘b6

In the event of 17...c5 18.a4 Black would still have had some problems with his queenside pawns. After the move in the game I thought that, since Black was not threatening to play ...c5 in the immediate future, and there were hardly any pieces left alongside his king, White would be able to develop an attack, but somehow it did not work out for me. I think that Black is now close to equality.

18.♕e3!

After other continuations Black plays ...♕e7 and then ...c5, for example: 18.♖ac1 ♕e7 19.c4 bxc4 20.♗xc4 c5 21.dxc5 ♘d7 – the c-pawn is regained,

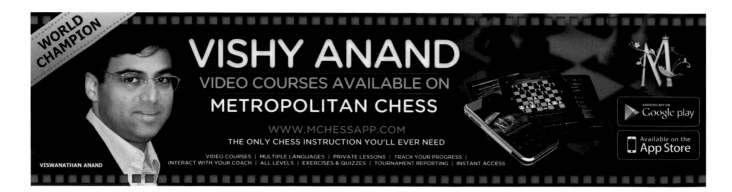

and the game should end in a draw. With the queen move White maintains the tension. I was expecting the reply 18...♕e7 and was intending to play on the kingside – 19.g4 with the idea of g5, or perhaps 19.♘e5, planning a pawn roller – f4, g4 and so on. The position is complicated, and Black has his chances.

18...♘a4

For some reason Dmitry made this move very quickly, although in my view it is a very responsible decision. At the board the knight manoeuvre seemed dubious to me, but the computer agrees more with my opponent, reckoning that Black maintains equality.

19.♗c2 ♘b2

20.♖db1!

It was because of this set-up that Black's venture seemed artificial to me. If 20.♖e1 he succeeds in playing 20...♘c4 21.♕e2 c5 with quite a decent game.

20...♘c4 21.♕c1

The placing of the white pieces looks strange, but Black is not able to prevent the move a4, and then the rooks will turn out to be on precisely the right squares. I assumed that the pressure on the b5-pawn would give White at least a small advantage. Of course, when you begin looking at the game with a computer, you are not able to demonstrate anything – it defends brilliantly.

21...c5

21...f5!? is interesting – such a 'ragged' move. I only noticed it in passing. 22.♘d2 ♘xd2 23.♕xd2 ♗xe4 leads to equality.

It seemed to me that after 22.exf5 exf5 23.a4 Black might have some problems with his queenside, but the machine finds some crazy resources, involving 23...f4. I will not give the variations it considers – they are lengthy and complicated, typically computer variations, and in the end approximate equality is reached. Of course, 21...c5 is a more sensible continuation.

22.a4 cxd4 23.cxd4 ♖c8 24.axb5 axb5

25.♕e1

A very important move. It is only thanks to it that White is able to retain some pressure, as otherwise he is simply unable to arrange his pieces. For example, 25.♖xb5 ♘d6 26.♖c5 ♗xe4 is an immediate draw.

25.♕e1 is the only possibility of creating play, although, I have to admit, I was very happy with my position: all my pieces stand well, and the b5-pawn is after all rather weak. My human assessment was that White has a stable plus, although the computer maintains equality relatively easily.

25...♗c6

Black wants to exchange one pair of rooks by ...♖a8, after which White's potential is significantly reduced. For example, after 26.♗d3 ♖a8 27.♖c1 ♖xa1 28.♖xa1 ♕b6 29.♖c1 ♖a8 he cannot count on anything.

Therefore I consider my next move to be a good one.

26.♖b4! ♖a8 27.♖d1

White is beginning to seriously threaten d5, but Dmitry finds a very powerful defensive resource.

The Tromsø World Cup was a great success largely due to the fabulous performance of Vladimir Kramnik. Staying focussed for a full three weeks, he proved that knock-out events can have deserved winners.

27...♖a3!

An unusual regrouping. Black intends to play ...♕a8, defending against the advance of the d-pawn with this rather strange manoeuvre and beginning to put pressure on White's centre. Here I realized that I had to act very quickly, as otherwise Black would gain comfortable play. After 28.♗b3 ♕a8 he has no problems at all.

28.d5!

The breakthrough can be carried out only now, exploiting the slight lack of harmony in the placing of the enemy pieces.

Already at this point I noticed the idea of the queen sacrifice. Objectively the assessment does not change, but Black has practical problems.

28...exd5 29.exd5 ♖e8

29...♗d7 does not look very good, but again only until you begin analys-

ing the position with a computer. It seemed to me that 30.♕e4 was dangerous, and if 30...g6, then 31.♕f4 ♔g7 32.♗d3, and White has a very serious initiative, while if 30...f5, then both 31.♕d4 and 31.♕f4 are possible. However, after 31.♕d4 ♕a5 32.♖db1 ♕a7, with the help of 'semi-tactical' tricks Black holds on. Of course, a human player wants to play 29...♖e8.

30.dxc6!

This is the whole point. 30.♕f1 is clearly not an option. After 30...♗d7 31.♗d3 ♘d6 only Black can play for a win. Dmitry either underestimated the queen sacrifice, or he altogether overlooked it. After this he began thinking seriously, whereas on the series of moves from 18...♘a4 to 27...♖a3 (incidentally, a very

good series) he only used about three minutes!

30...♖xe1+

31.♘xe1!

31.♖xe1 results in a forced draw: 31...g6 32.♖xb5 ♕c3 33.♖c5 ♕d6 34.♖e8+ ♔g7 35.c7 ♕xc5 36.c8♕ ♕xc8 37.♖xc8 ♖xc2 – the tactical skirmish has led to the complete exhaustion of the forces. The idea was to capture with the knight. It is possible that in advance Dmitry had not seen that if 31...♕b6 there is 32.♖xb5!.

31...♕c7 The correct reply.

32.♖xb5

I tried calculating variations such as 32.♖d7 ♕c8 33.♗f5, but nothing comes of this. White has a draw, but there is no question of a win.

32...g6

Forced, to avoid being mated.

33.♖c5

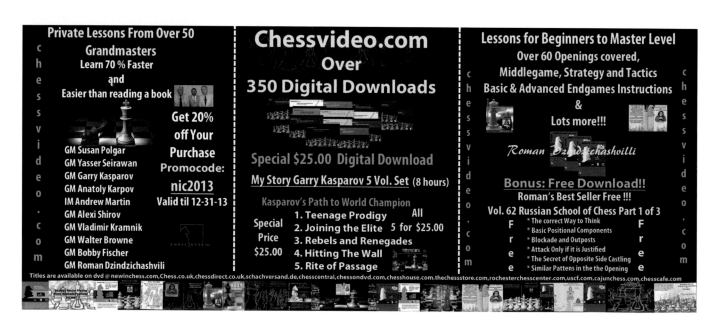

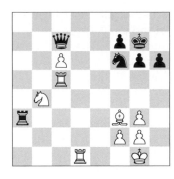

When I played 28.d5 I aimed roughly for this position, reckoning that Black would not immediately pick up the c6-pawn. For a human player it is obvious that only two results are possible. The probability of a draw is far higher than the probability of White winning, but even so he is playing without the slightest risk, whereas for Black there certainly is a risk. The computer does not realize this and it gives 'dead level' after almost every move. In fact I was happy about how the situation had changed. In view of Black's imminent time-trouble, it is not so easy to defend here.

33...♘e5 As Black I would probably also have played this: one wants to post the knight in the centre and 'half-attack' the c6-pawn, plus moving to g4 may create some threats to the king.

It is hard to think of a more natural move, but strangely the computer insists that 33...♘d6 was more accurate. Few would make this move: the knight's position is rather hanging. The idea, as I understand it, is that at some point Black may want to regroup with ...♘e8 and after the queen moves – ...♘c7. All the same I do not agree with these 'dead levels': after 33...♘d6 34.♖c1 ♖a2 35.♗d3 White is playing for a win. The position is close to a draw, but nevertheless it is not equal.

33...♘e5 is the first of a series of minor inaccuracies, which in the end lead to defeat. Even after analysis it is hard to understand where Black really went wrong. For me this is an indication of the quality of the game, and therefore I am happy with it.

34.♗e4 ♘g4 Again a slightly unfortunate, but perfectly understandable move. 34...♖a4, dislodging the bishop, was rather more accurate, although after 35.♗d5 I do not see a constructive plan for Black. White will probably play ♘f3, exchange knights and gradually transfer his rook to b7. The computer holds the position thanks to little tactics, such as perpetual checks, but for a human it is very unpleasant. With the move in the game Black wants to create counterplay, but White finds a very strong reply.

35.♘d3! Cutting off the black knight, which does not have a strong point. Another significant drawback of Black's position is his blockading queen, as we all know from back in the pioneers' palace.

35...♔g7 36.♗f3 ♘f6 Certainly not 36...h5 37.♗xg4 hxg4 38.♖c4 ♖a8 39.♘f4, when the knight goes to d5. Generally speaking, with the knight this position is even more difficult for Black than with the bishop.

37.♘b4

It is obvious that White has made some progress, but it is still difficult to win. The move made by me is logical. On the one hand, it denies Black the possibility of ...♖a2 (although I am not sure that this is such a big threat), but the main idea is to exchange the knight on d5 and obtain the desired position. It was also possible to go via f4.

37...h5
A sensible time-trouble move.

38.♖dc1 ♖a7 39.♘d5
Here I thought for a long time. I wanted to transfer my rook via b5 to b7, but it didn't work. I decided nevertheless to exchange the knight.

39...♘xd5 40.♗xd5

40...♕d8

I was fortunate that Black had to take a very important decision on the 40th move, and Dmitry had just a couple of minutes left. If now Black does not move his queen from c7, he, so to speak, will never move it. White is threatening to play ♗f3, after which the queen will remain the blockader for ever. It is another matter that all the same it is very difficult to break this blockade. I was also most concerned about 40...♕d8, and in this respect I thought like Dmitry: there is a brief instant 'between the past and the future', and Black must seize the opportunity to move the queen and replace it with the rook on c7. But, I repeat, the decision is a highly responsible one, since Black has to reckon with the consequences of c6-c7.

As it transpired in analysis, Black should have played 40...f5, and if 41. ♗f3 – 41...♔h6!, and simply stood his ground. Outwardly the position seems very dangerous, but in fact it is not lost. Perhaps it makes sense for White to play 42.♖5c4, taking control of the h4-square, and then ♔h2... But the direct attempt 42.♖b5 (with the idea of ♖cb1 and ♖b7) is parried by the cool computer move 42...♕g7!, and if 43. ♖b7, then 43...♖a1!. In the variation 43.♔h2 ♖c7 44.♖d1 ♕e7 45.♖b7 h4! Black succeeds in creating counterplay: 46.gxh4 ♕xh4+ 47.♔g1 ♖c8. But even if not in time-trouble, it would be very difficult to take such a decision.

In the event of 41.♖b5 ♖c7 42.♖b7, despite the fact that Black has managed to regroup, his position is quite unpleasant. But here I saw a tactical possibility, which my opponent had obviously underestimated.

41.c7!
Here Dmitry thought for a very long time, although there is strictly only one reply. It was apparent that he had not expected this move at all.
41...♖xc7 The pawn cannot be allowed to remain on c7.

42.♖xc7 ♕xd5

43.♖e1! Of course, the endgame would be drawn, were it not for this very important move. For tactical reasons Black cannot retain the f7-g6-h5 pawn chain, and he is forced to weaken himself. Now White's position, if not won, is very close to this. At any event, in analysis I have been unable to find a clear way for Black to hold on.
43...♔h6 Evidently the only move. It is important that the 'three against two' pawn endgame, arising in vari-

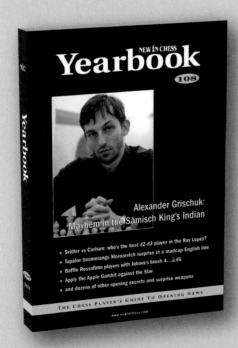

ous versions, is won (at least with the pawn on f2). For example, 43...♔f8 44.♖ee7 ♕f5 45.♖xf7+ ♕xf7 46. ♖xf7+ ♔xf7 47.♔h2 (the simplest) 47...♔f6 48.♔h3 g5 49.g4 h4 50.f4. Then White places his pawn on f5 and his king goes right round the board.

44.♖ee7

The doubled pawns defend the king well, and Black can never give perpetual check.

44...f6

Also a rather dismal move, but it has to be made, since it is clear that after 44...f5 45.f4 ♕g8 Black cannot save the game by keeping his queen on g8 and h8. After 46.♖f7 ♕h8 47.♔h2 ♕g8 48.♖cd7 ♕h8 49.♖d6 White gradually wins the f5-pawn.

45.♖ed7!

A very unpleasant move for Black. If 45.f4 there would have followed 45... g5, and here I do not see a direct win. The queen is occupying an excellent square in the middle of the board. After slightly weighing up the variations, I realized that it had to be dislodged.

Andreikin thought for almost all of his remaining time and, it would seem, made the strongest move (the first line of the computer), although it is probably no longer possible to save the game.

45...♕a5

I thought that there were still some chances in the event of 45...♕e4. In fact after 46.♖h7+ ♔g5 47.♖c5+ f5 48.♔h2 (we both considered this to be the strongest continuation for White) White gradually picks up the g6-pawn: 48...♕e1 (a counterattack-

The winner with a small trophy and a big cheque. First prize minus FIDE tax was $96,000 and like anyone else Vladimir Kramnik had to pay his own expenses.

ing attempt: 48...♔f6 49.f4) 49.♖c6 ♕xf2 50.♖g7 f4 51.♖gxg6+ ♔f5 52. ♖cf6+ ♔e5 53.♖xf4 ♕d2 54.♖g5+ ♔e6 55.♖xh5.

I will give another variation, one which is very pretty from the geometric point of view: 45...♕b5 46.f4 (there are also other possibilities, but I like the way that the computer takes Black's position apart – quite brilliantly, in my view) 46...♕b1+ 47.♔h2 g5 48.♖f7 ♔g6 49.♖g7+ ♔h6 50.fxg5+ fxg5 51.♖gd7 ♕g6 52.♖d8 ♕e6 53.♖dc8 ♕e4 54.♖c6+ ♔g7 55. ♖8c7+ ♔g8 56.♖d6 ♕e8 57.♖dd7 h4 58.♖g7+ ♔f8

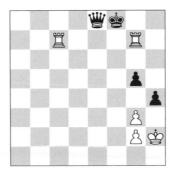

ANALYSIS DIAGRAM

59.♖cf7+ ♕xf7 60.♖xf7+ ♔xf7 61. gxh4 gxh4 62.♔h3.

46.f4 g5 47.♔h2

After 47.♖h7+ ♔g6 48.♖cg7+ ♔f5 it is not so easy to win. After 49.fxg5 fxg5 there is not 50.♖xh5 on account of 50...♕a1+ 51.♔h2 ♕xg7 – this is the idea of 45...♕a5. 49.♖xh5 is possible, but after 49...♕e1+ 50.♔h2 ♕e8 51.♖gh7 ♔g4 no direct win is apparent, and it will be not so easy to pick up the g5-pawn.

Therefore I made another stealthy move, after which 47...gxf4 is not possible in view of 48.♖h7+ ♔g6 49.♖cg7+ ♔f5 50.♖xh5+ ♔e6 51.♖xa5 – here the drawbacks to the queen's position on a5 are seen!

47...♔g6

The only move.

48.fxg5

We both thought that this position was completely hopeless. Strangely enough, when I analysed it with the computer, I discovered that after 48...fxg5! Black still retains some practical chances. For example, I thought that after 49.♖d6+ ♔f5 50.♖f7+ ♔e5 51.♖h6 h4 52.gxh4 I would pick up both pawns, but the computer plays 52...♕d2 and by some miracle it does not give up the second. Thus Black could have reached the endgame with two rooks and g-pawn against queen. I have no doubt that it is objectively won, and nevertheless, as I understand it, here I would have had to include my king in the play. A similar ending was won by Karpov against Anand in the first game of their match in Lausanne, in 1998.

48...♔xg5

This move can be regarded as the decisive mistake. Now by shuttle manoeuvres with the rooks I win both pawns, and my king is not needed.

49.♖h7 f5 50.♖cg7+ ♔f6

51.♖a7!

An important manoeuvre, leading to the fall of the h5-pawn.

51...♕b4

Dmitry was already totally disheartened. He should have played 51...♕e5, deferring for some time the fall of the f5-pawn. Of course, after 52.♖xh5 ♔g6 53.♖h4 all the same I pick it up with my rooks, seeing as any pawn endgames with two g-pawns are won.

52.♖a6+ ♔e5 53.♖xh5

Here the pawn is lost immediately.

53...♕b1 54.♖a5+ ♔f6 55. ♖axf5+ ♔g6

White has a simple plan: with the help of checks and attacks on the queen he drives the king to the edge of the board and gives mate.

56.♖fg5+ ♔f6 57.♖b5 ♕c2 58. ♖h6+ ♔g7 59.♖bb6 ♕c5 60. ♖bg6+ ♔f8 61.♖h7 ♕f5 62.♖gg7 ♕e6 63.♖e7

The queen is dislodged from the e-file – the only one on which it was still possible somehow to hold on. If 63...♕d6 there follows 64.♖d7 ♕f6 65.♖d8+ ♕xd8 66.♖h8+.
Black resigned.

Afterwards I came to the conclusion that this was a game of very high quality, in which Black defended very well, and simply things did not quite work out for him. So I am pleased not only because I was able to win this game, which became decisive in the battle for the World Cup, but also because it proved a very worthy one.

■ ■ ■

For the legitimacy of the World Cup, Kramnik certainly was a worthy winner. The cup format has been criticized for being random and just a big gamble, but it's good to see that pure playing strength beats all of this.

Tromsø 2013	
7 rounds of knock-oout	
Round 3	
Aronian-Tomashevsky	½-1½
Malakhov-Caruana	1-3
Kramnik-Areshchenko	3-1
Le Quang Liem-Grischuk	2½-1½
Karjakin-Eljanov	4½-3½
Adhiban-Nakamura	0-2
Gelfand-Moiseenko	1½-½
Hammer-Kamsky	½-1½
Mamedyarov-Wei Yi	2½-1½
Vachier-Lagrave-Dominguez	1½-½
Dubov-Korobov	1½-2½
Andreikin-Dreev	4-2
Svidler-Radjabov	1½-½
Ivanchuk-Kryvoruchko	3-1
Granda Zuniga-Giri	2½-1½
Vitiugov-Morozevich	3½-4½
Round 4	
Morozevich-Tomashevsky	3½-4½
Caruana-Granda Zuniga	2-0
Ivanchuk-Kramnik	½-1½
Le Quang Liem-Svidler	1½-2½
Andreikin-Karjakin	3-1
Nakamura-Korobov	½-1½
Vachier-Lagrave-Gelfand	2½-1½
Kamsky-Mamedyarov	1½-½
Round 5 Quarter Finals	
Tomashevsky-Kamsky	1½-½
Vachier-Lagrave-Caruana	2½-1½
Kramnik-Korobov	1½-½
Andreikin-Svidler	2½-1½
Round 6 Semi-Finals	
Andreikin-Tomashevsky	2½-1½
Vachier-Lagrave-Kramnik	1½-2½
Final	
Kramnik-Andreikin	2½-1½

To me, after following this tournament a little more closely than usual, the main harvest is all the great games and struggles. For a chess enthusiast the World Cup is a mental delicacy that can be chewed on long after the curtain has fallen. The games are all there! We just scraped a little off the top of an iceberg in this article. There were disasters (like myself) and winners, but all in all this was a fantastic show! ■

Beware: Brilliancy!

Oversights are part of the practice of each and every one of us. A great majority of them bear no special interest beyond the obvious lesson to avoid repeating them. All six positions below are culled from the games of the contenders in the forthcoming World Championship match. Apparently they are human too, even if of a different level.

★★ ★★★

1. Black to play

With the careless **35...♖xf6** Black exposed his monarch, allowing **36.♕c3 ♔g7 37.♕g3+ ♔g6 38.♕e5+! ♖f6 39.♕g5+ ♔g6 40.♕e5+ ♔f8** with a perpetual. Was there a better option?

★★★ ★★

2. White to play

White continued his attack with the natural looking **28.♘xe5**, which ran into the counterblow **28...♕xe3!** White had only considered 28...♖d6?? 29.♖xd6 cxd6 30.♘d4!. **29.♘xd7 ♖h8!** Threatening 30...♕e1!. **30.♔g2 ♖h3 31.♗xg6! ♘xg6 32.♔f1?** ♖h1+ and Black won. Did White have a better choice?

★★★ ★★

3. Black to play

Black has just sacrificed a rook on d5 and continued **14...♕e4** which allowed White to consolidate with **15.♔e2!**. After hair-raising complications (and errors!) the game eventually ended peacefully. What did Black miss in the diagrammed position?

★★★★ ★

4. White to play

White played the trivial **18.♗d2**, but after 18...♖h4 19.♖f1 ♗f6 20.♖ae1 ♗xe5 21.♗h7+ ♔h8 22.♖xf8+ ♕xf8 23.♖xe5 ♘c4! 24.♖xh5 ♘xd2 25.♕xd2 dxc3! 26.♕xc3 there was nothing much to play for. Do you spot a less trivial idea?

★★★ ★★

5. Black to play

The black pieces seem more active and he went on to win with the solid **25...exd3 26.♗xd3 ♗xd3 27.♖xd3 c5 28.♗e5 ♖xd3 29.♗xb8 c4!**, forcing White's resignation on move 36. How could he have pleased the crowd?

★★★★★

6. White to play

White set a naive trap: **27.♖g1**, hoping for the cheap 27...♕xf4? 28.♖d4, but needed another 30 moves to convert his advantage. Was there a more forcing and attractive alternative?

The number of stars roughly indicates their estimated level of difficulty: 1 is easiest and 5 most difficult.   **Solutions on page 129**

Voyages of Discovery

The holiday period has not been very restful for me. Too many projects seem to have decided that 1st September would be a good time to go live! So arriving home battered, bruised and worn out, all I wanted in the evening was a bit of quiet and a good way to relax. Luckily for me, the solution came through the post: review books from New In Chess! I had the feeling that the first book I unpacked would become a constant companion and that proved to be the case: *Study Chess with Mikhail Tal* (Mikhail Tal & Alexander Koblencs). This is a reprint of a book first published in Germany in 1978. It's not that the book itself is so fantastic – the layout looks extremely old-fashioned, the comments by Koblencs are fine but nothing amazing – but the games, ah the games...!

In his strangely thought-provoking book *Best Play. A New Method For Discovering The Strongest Move* (which I'll review fully in a few issues' time – I need some time to get my head around the concepts!) the Russian author Alexander Shashin describes the 4 elements of what he calls the 'Tal Algorithm':

1. *Open* (one-move) and *direct* (two-move) attacks on our opponent's material chess targets

2. The optimal arrangement of our pieces on squares conducive to subsequent open or direct attacks on our opponent's material chess targets

3. The sacrifice of chess material (we sacrifice material in order to increase the tempo of attack)

4. Winning chess material.

In other words, Tal is always either attacking the opponent's pawns and pieces, or bringing his pieces to squares from which he can attack his opponent's pawns and pieces.

That's not quite as stating the obvious as it seems! After reading that little paragraph, a couple of fragments from *Study Chess with Mikhail Tal* suddenly popped into my mind.

Here's the culmination of the attack in Tal-Furman, Riga 1956. Guess the moves!

21.♖f5! Hitting the queen on a5 and the loose rook on h8. **21...e5**

Study Chess with Tal
Based on diaries
kept by Tal's coach
Alexander Koblencs
by Mikhail Tal &
Alexander Koblencs
Batsford, 2013

22.♕a7! Hitting the loose rook on b8, when **22...♕b6 23.♕xb6+ ♖xb6 24.♘d5 ♗xf5 25.exf5 ♖b8 26.f6 ♗f8 27.axb4** was catastrophic for Black. In 2 moves, Tal attacked Black's queen and both Black's rooks! And here's the start of the attack:

12.♗d2! Attacking the black queen. **12...♕a6 13.♘f5!** Attacking the loose bishop on e7. **13...♗d8** Once you start noticing it, it really is striking how many of Tal's attacks exploit unprotected pieces. In this game Tal generated momentum at the start of an attack by first knocking pieces off their best squares (♘f5 pushes the bishop back to d8, slicing Black's position in two by cutting off the connection between Black's queenside and kingside) and then by freeing a square necessary for the attack with tempo (but did you spot that ♗d2 was freeing g5 for the queen?). In the game against Furman, Tal kept his attack going with constant hits against the opponent's unprotected (heavy) pieces. It's just normal attacking technique of course, but I don't think I'd ever consciously thought about it until I saw these games!

Another very instructive part to the book is the triptych of games starting from this position:

This is nothing less than a complete textbook for how to attack an untouched kingside pawn structure (f7, g7, h7) with pawns on h4 and g5. Tal went 15.g6 of course and in the course of his career, he faced all 3 possibilities: taking with the f-pawn, taking with the h-pawn and just ignoring it! Taking with the h-pawn led to the immortal game Tal-Koblencs. If you haven't seen it, then I'll give you a diagram as a taster!

Leaving it led to the very nice game Tal-Stoltz in 1959. The capture with the f-pawn led to this wonderful attack:

SI 28.2 – B63
Mikhail Tal
Dieter Mohrlok
Varna Olympiad 1962

1.e4 c5 2.♘f3 ♘c6 3.d4 cxd4 4. ♘xd4 ♘f6 5.♘c3 d6 6.♗g5 e6 7.♕d2 ♗e7 8.0-0-0 0-0 9.♘b3 ♕b6 10.f3 a6 11.g4 ♖d8 12.♗e3 ♕c7 13.g5 ♘d7 14.h4 b5
This position has occurred a number of times since 1957, and it's funny to

look at the strong players who didn't play 15.g6! Vishy Anand played 15.♔b1 against Andrew Muir in 1993, while Peter Svidler could only muster 15.h5 against Xu Jun in 2001. Even our own mad hacker Stuart Conquest played the mysterious 15.♕g2 !
15.g6 fxg6 16.h5 gxh5 17.♖xh5 ♘f6

18.♖g5 I love this move. Nigel Short played the more natural 18.♖h1 against Andrew Muir (him again!) at Gibraltar in 2004 and won convincingly with a massive build-up of forces on the kingside.
18.♖g5 is probably not stronger, but shows fine attacking awareness by switching White's attention to the kingside pawn that is defended only by the black king. Strangely enough, this wasn't Tal's idea! Spassky had played this against Boleslavsky in 1958 already.
18...♘e5 19.♕g2 ♗f8 20.♗e2
Here Tal deviates from the aforementioned Spassky game (Spassky played the equally sensible 20.f4 though he went completely bananas a few moves later and was extremely lucky to draw).
20...♘c4 21.♗xc4 bxc4 22.♘d4 ♖b8

And now see if you can guess Tal's idea. I didn't see it coming at all!
23.♖h1 ♖b7 24.♖h6

Such a great idea: no stereotyped tripling on the g-file for Tal! It is what Shashin calls a direct (2-move) attack on the opponent's pieces. It wasn't too easy to spot though that the knight on f6 was loose!
24...♔f7 25.♖h4 ♕b6 26.♘d1 ♕c7 27.f4 h6 28.♖g6 ♖e8 29.f5 e5 30.♘c3!!

Wonderful! 30...exd4 31.♖xf6+ gxf6 32.♘d5 with 33.♕g6 mate to follow.
30...♕d8 31.♘c6
A 1-move attack on the queen to finish! Once the queen leaves d8, ♖xf6+ is decisive. Black resigned.

Fantastic fun! If you don't have a book of Tal's games, then this one is definitely a worthwhile start.

Ivanchuk

Another book that's been keeping me company the past month is *Vassily Ivanchuk 100 Selected Games* by Nikolay Kalinichenko. I am so happy

Sadler on Books

I didn't get this book before having to play Vassily in May: this guy is good! You get such a weird feeling playing through these games: it's barely conceivable that the same player has played them. There are controlled technical wins, crazy attacks, completely irrational sacrifices, brilliant opening concepts. And that's before you count in the staggering breadth of his opening repertory. So impressive!

I could delectate you with thousands of moments, here are just a few that stuck in my mind.

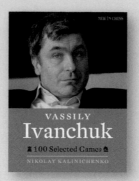

Vassily Ivanchuk
100 Selected Games
by Nikolay Kalinichenko
New In Chess, 2013

position kind of looks like a Tal position, doesn't it?

17.♘ec4 ♕c7 18.♖he1 b5 19. ♘e3 ♖xa2 20.♕b3 ♖a4 21.♖e2 ♕a7 22.♘ef5+ ♔d8 23.♘xf7+ ♖xf7 24.♕xe6 ♘b6 25.b3 White resigned.

Bruzon-Ivanchuk
Havana 2011
position after 12.♗d2

The concept Ivanchuk applies here is well-known, but not in such an accelerated form!

12...a5 13.0-0-0 ♗b4! 14.♗xb4 axb4 15.♘d6+ ♔e7 16.♘e5 ♖f8

Yep, this works for Black! King in the centre, a nice quiet defensive move to defend an attacked pawn... and Black is better (the white a-pawn is hanging, as well as the knight on d6). White's

Aronian-Ivanchuk
Sao Paulo/Bilbao Grand Slam Final 2011
position after 16.f4

The battle is hotting up. Aronian lost time in the opening with an original ♘f3-d2-f3 manoeuvre, but on the other hand this meant that he didn't have time to commit his king to the queenside!

16...c5 17.f5 cxd4 18.fxe6 dxc3 19.0-0 d4 20.♘xf7 ♕d5 21.♗xf6 ♕h1+ 22.♔f2 ♕xh3

A quite incredible resource, stopping 23.♘h6 mate while threatening 23...♕xe3 mate.

23.♔e1 cxb2!
Opening the a5-e1 diagonal for the dark-squared bishop.

24.♕xb2 ♗b4+ 25.♔d1 ♗f3+ 26.♖xf3 ♕xf3+ 27.♗e2 ♕xf6 28. g5 ♕g7 29.♕xd4 ♖xf7 30.exf7+ ♕xf7 31.♖c1 ♖b8 32.a4 ♕b3+ 33.♖c2 ♕b1+ 34.♖c1 ♕b3+ 35. ♖c2 ♖c8 36.♗c4+ bxc4 37.♕d5+ ♔f8 38.♕d7 ♖e8 White resigned.
I really have had a great time playing through this. The annotations are informative and quite easy to read despite occasional dense thickets of analysis when Ivanchuk plunges into something incomprehensible! Recommended!

Garry Kasparov

And so we come to the next instalment of Garry's magisterial review of the World Champions and his own career: *Garry Kasparov on Garry Kasparov Part II: 1985-1993*. Again really good! And yet... somewhere a slight feeling of disappointment crept over me when reading the book. I couldn't place it at first but I think it came from the fact that without exception, I had seen all the games before! Both the Ivanchuk book and the Tal book gave you a feeling of being on a voyage of discovery which made them easy to get into without much effort. The novelty in this book lies hidden in the notes, in the reappraisal of *Informator* variations with the computer, the comments of other annotators in the intervening years and the games since played in the

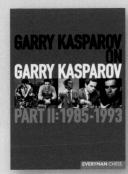

Garry Kasparov
on Garry
Kasparov - Part II
1985-1993
by Garry Kasparov
Everyman Chess,
2013

opening variations. But once you get into that, there is plenty of wonderful insight and analysis to keep you going for the next few years. One thing that caught my eye was a triad of games with a very similar theme. Again, just as with the Tal examples mentioned before, you could build a textbook on how to handle these types of positions just by studying these games.

Kasparov-Hübner
Brussels 1986
position after 15...♗e7

16.♗g5 ♗xg5 17.♘xg5 ♘f6 18. ♖d1 ♗e6 19.♖e1 ♕d8 20.♘xe6 fxe6

Kasparov-COMP Deep Blue
Philadelphia 1996 (4)
position after 15...♘f6

16.♗e3 ♗xe3 17.♖xe3 ♗g4 18. ♘e5 ♖e8 19.♖ae1 ♗e6 20.f4

Kasparov-Karpov
Amsterdam 1988 (4)
position after 15...♕e7

16.♗f4
Kasparov puts it this way:
'The same motifs are evident as in my games with Hübner and Deep Blue: the exchange of the dark-squared bishops, the development of the queen's rook with gain of tempo, and the aim of obtaining light-squared bishop against knight with the better pawn structure.'
16...♗xf4 17.♕xf4 ♘f8 18.♖e1 ♗e6 19.♘d4 ♖d8 20.h4 ♕c5 21. ♖e3 ♕d6 22.♘xe6 fxe6

What's really funny is that there is once again a triad of games in this structure with an isolated e-pawn:

Kasparov-Hübner
Brussels 1986
position after 20...fxe6

21.♕e3 ♔h8 22.h3 ♕d7 23.g4 ♖e8 24.♕e5 ♕d8 25.♔g2 ♕b6 26.♖d1 c5 27.a4 ♖f8 28.♖d6

♕c7 29.♖xe6 ♕f7 30.♕xc5 ♘xg4 31.♕xf8+ ♕xf8 32.hxg4 Black resigned.

Kasparov-Karpov
Amsterdam 1988 (4)
after 22... fxe6

Kasparov-Karpov
Seville 1987 (24)
position after 40.♕xb6

Slightly different, but nonetheless showing definite similarities to the first games.

Hübner lost his position very quickly whereas Karpov held his for many hours. What is the difference? Kasparov explains it like this: 'An analogous pawn structure, with similar material, was soon to arise in two of my games with Karpov but there the knight was better-placed – on f8, defending the e6-pawn and the weakened light-squares.'

So once again warmly recommended: lots of good stuff to learn from all this. I'm really looking forward to the next instalment covering the great games against Nigel in 1993! ∎

Hou Yifan routs Ushenina to regain title

In New In Chess 2011/6, I discussed the possibility of Hou Yifan following in Judit Polgar's footsteps. It seemed to me that a match between these two stars would make for an interesting clash. Then Hou Yifan's development seemed to stagnate. For two years, she failed to score any wins capable of firing people's imagination. In Wijk aan Zee this year, she showed that she could beat even the strongest grandmasters, but then she went on to disappoint in the Women's Grand Prix tournament in Geneva. I read a poll somewhere about the question of whether Hou Yifan might grow as strong as Judit Polgar. Most of the respondents said no. But Hou Yifan's convincing victory in her World Championship match against Ushenina has changed the situation

ANASTASIYA KARLOVICH

With a rating difference of more than 100 points there was little doubt who was the favourite in the Women's World Championship match in Taizhou. Still, there was little reason to believe that World Champion Anna Ushenina would stand absolutely no chance to cling on to her title. Winning three consecutive black games, Hou Yifan essentially decided the issue in only one week. The final blow was dealt in Game 7, ending the 10-game match eight days after it had started with a telling 5½-1½ score. The inevitable next question is what Hou Yifan's chances would be in a match against Judit Polgar. Jan Timman believes that the moment has come for the Chinese grandmaster to seek this challenge.

all over again. Judit would not have improved on her result.

Hou Yifan started the match as a modest favourite because of her clearly higher rating. As against this, their encounter in Geneva was won by Ushenina. Both players went on to participate in the World Cup in Tromsø, which started exactly one month before their match. It turned out to be a good final rehearsal for both of them. In the classical games, Ushenina scored 1-1 against Peter Svidler, before she was eliminated in the rapid tiebreak, while Hou Yifan did the same against Alexey Shirov, who failed to get anywhere in either of the games.

The world championship match was played in the southern Chinese city of Taizhou, near Xinghao, the city where Hou Yifan was born and raised, so it was a home game for her. This is not necessarily an advantage. Anand is in the same position, playing Carlsen in Chennai. Hou Yifan, incidentally, must have been pretty startled when she saw grandmasters Khalifman and Korobov descend on her so familiar turf. Ushenina had an extremely

Blissfully ignorant of the things to come, a smiling Anna Ushenina shows that she will play with the white pieces in the first game.

strong team of seconds. What did Hou Yifan have to set against this? Khalifman did not see any other strong grandmasters in Taizhou, but after the match he nevertheless said: 'We didn't have the slightest doubt that Hou Yifan was getting help from a very strong team as well. This preparation of hers in the Perenyi Attack against the Najdorf. It was clear that she had not been preparing with her mom and dad.'

Hou Yifan told a very different story

after the match, emphasizing that her first college term had started and that she had had too little time for a thorough preparation. It was only after her return from Tromsø that she had engaged someone – no name provided, but both GM Zhou Weiqi and GM Yu Shaoteng, with whom she has worked before and who appeared in the playing hall, were suggested – to prepare for the match.

The striking thing was that Hou Yifan's victory was mainly based on her wins as Black, despite the fact that her Black repertoire used to be somewhat shaky. What happened in the first game was of great importance.

Ushenina-Hou Yifan
Taizhou 2013 (1)
position after 25...♗e6

The first, and possibly last, critical moment in the match. With 26.♘xb5! White could have grabbed an advantage. After 26...♛xb5 27.♘xe7+ ♚h8 28.♘d5 White has the position under control. The black knight is very badly positioned on b7. This is quite obvious, and I think that Ushenina had made an understandable error in her calculations here. After 26...♜b3 27.♘c7! ♜xb1 28.♘xe8 ♜xc1 White has the intermediate move 29.♘xe7+, with a winning advantage.
26.♘xe7+ ♛xe7 27.♘d5 ♘xd5 28.exd5

Black has the same position now, in fact, as in the comments to White's 26th move, except with an extra pawn on b5. But White still has compensation in view of the bad position of the black knight.
28...♗g4 29.♜d2 f5
True to form, Hou Yifan goes for the

attack. More cautious natures might have gone for 29...♜fa8, or even 29...♜b8 to cover the b-pawn preventively.
30.♜dc2 f4

31.♜c7
A counterattack that will yield preciously little.
The critical move was 31.gxf4, intending to meet 31...exf4 with 32.♗d4. Stronger is 31...♗f5. After 32.♛b2 ♜xe3! Black remains better.
31...♛f6 32.♗b6 ♘d8
Another possibility was 32...♘c5 to block the diagonal of the white queen's bishop. But Hou Yifan has a clear plan: she wants to transfer the badly placed black knight to the kingside to assist in the attack.
33.♛b2 ♜d3

34.♛c2
In raging time-trouble, Ushenina misses her best chance. With 34.♗e4 White could have limited the damage. Now the black attack is given wings.
34...♗f5 35.♛a2 ♘f7
On its way to g5. It is fascinating to see how the black knight, so awkwardly placed on the queenside, will eventually play a leading role in the attack.
36.♗f1 ♘g5 37.♜a7

37...fxg3 38.hxg3 ♘f3+
Now White will inevitably get mated in short order.
39.♚h1 ♛g6 40.♗xd3 ♛h5+ 41.♚g2 ♗h3+ White resigned.

In the second game, Hou Yifan was surprised by the Sveshnikov; Ushenina usually plays the Najdorf. In such a situation you should take things easy as White, especially if you're leading. Hou Yifan's play was exemplary. After 33 moves an otherwise uneventful game ended in a draw. In Game 3, Hou Yifan struck again with the black pieces.

NI 24.13 – E32
Anna Ushenina
Hou Yifan
Taizhou 2013 (3)

1.d4 ♘f6 2.c4 e6 3.♘c3 ♗b4 4.♛c2 0-0 5.e4

This advance is enjoying some popularity, although I don't really understand why. If Black plays solidly, White has very little hope of an advantage.
5...d5 6.e5 ♘e4 7.♗d3 c5 8.♘f3 cxd4 9.♘xd4 ♘d7 10.♗f4

10...♘dc5

With 10...♕h4 Black could have gone for a sharper fight, but the text is entirely justified strategically.

11.0-0 ♗xc3 12.bxc3 ♗d7

The alternative 12...b6 is more common here, forcing White to swap on d5.

But the text seems more logical to me. Black is ready to take her rook to c8, while at the same time taking control of square a4. This will become an important theme in the game.

13.♗e2 ♘a4 14.cxd5 exd5 15.c4 ♖c8

16.♕b3

Ushenina thought for a long time about this move, which is strange,

Hou Yifan arrives in the playing hall where Ye Jiangchuang, head coach of the Chinese Chess Association, and Yu Shaoteng, with whom she worked on earlier occasions, are already waiting. On the left chief arbiter Carol Jarecki.

since this is still a theoretical position in which White has tried various moves. In summary:

A) 16.♗d3 b5!, with excellent play for Black (Mekhitarian-Mareco, Moscow 2011)

B) 16.♖ab1 ♘b6 17.f3 ♘c5, with sufficient counterplay for Black (Sarkar-Gelashvili, Philadelphia World Open 2011)

C) 16.♖fe1! This is probably White's best option. The game Holt-Lenderman, Richardson 2012, continued as follows:

ANALYSIS DIAGRAM

16...b5 17.f3 ♘ec3, and now 18.cxb5! (instead of 18.♗d3) would have yielded White an advantage. Black's 16th move was too energetic for this

position. With 16...♕h4 17.g3 ♕e7 he would just have maintained the balance.

With the text White removes her queen from the pin, but at the expense of quite a bit of time.

16...dxc4

New. In Gundavaa-Alekseev, Kazan 2013, there followed 16...♘ac3 17. cxd5 ♗a4 18.♕xb7 ♖c7 19.♕a6 ♕xd5, with roughly equal chances. The text is more ambitious.

17.♗xc4?

This obvious recapture turns out to be the decisive mistake. White should have gone for 17.♕xb7, although this is obviously not in the spirit of White's play. After 17...♘ac5 18.♕b2 ♘d3 19.♗xd3 cxd3 20.♖fd1 ♘c5 the computer assesses the chances as equal, but in practice this position seems to me to be easier to play for Black.

17...♘ac3

Surprisingly enough, White is powerless here in the face of the deadly grip of the black knight pair. The threat is 18...♗a4.

18.a4

This won't help. White's best chance was 18.♗xf7+ ♖xf7 19.e6. White wins back the sacrificed piece immediately, but after 19...♗xe6 20.♘xe6 ♕f6 she will find it impossible to maintain the coordination between her pieces, e.g. 21.♖ae1 a5! 22.a4 ♘c6, and White has nothing better than 23.f3, after which Black can liquidate to a winning endgame with 23...♕xe6.

18...♗xa4!

Regardless!

19.♖xa4 ♘xa4

20.♘f5 After 20.♕xa4 ♘c3 21.♕b4 ♕xd4 22.♗xf7+ ♖xf7 23.♕xd4 ♘e2+ Black would win at once. The text is White's only chance.

20...♘ac3 The knight has returned to its post, and the grip of the knight pair is even more crippling than before.

21.e6

21...♖xc4! The most convincing way to win. **22.♕xc4 b5** The point of the previous move. The white queen is totally dominated by the black knights.

23.♕b3 ♕d3 24.exf7+ ♖xf7

White resigns. All her pieces are hanging.

After Game 4 there was a reversal of colours, with the result that Hou Yifan's next two games would be as White. In both games, Ushenina went for her tried and tested Najdorf Variation. This is understandable, as the Najdorf is more suited to a must-win situation than the Sveshnikov with its many forced lines. In Game 4, Hou Yifan initially got a favourable queenless middlegame, but after a few inaccuracies she lost her advantage. In Game 5, Ushenina had a chance to get an advantage, but when she missed it, the game again petered out in a draw. This meant that it was absolutely vital for Ushenina to win the sixth game.

QI 7.9 – E17
Anna Ushenina
Hou Yifan
Taizhou 2013 (6)

1.d4 ♘f6 2.c4 e6 3.♘f3

No Nimzo this time.

3...b6 4.g3 ♗b7 5.♗g2 ♗e7 6. ♘c3 0-0 7.♕c2 c5 8.d5 exd5 9. ♘h4

9...♘c6

With 9...b5 Black could have gone for a sharper battle. The text, which was already played in the 1930s, is based on a sound strategic plan.

10.cxd5 ♘d4 11.♕d1 ♘e8

The point. Black forces an exchange of knights and gets a playable Benoni position.

12.♘f3 ♘xf3+ 13.♗xf3 d6 14.0-0 ♘c7 15.a4 a6 16.♖b1

The start of a misconceived plan. White wants to meet the advance of the black b-pawn with b2-b4. In the Benoni this is a normal plan, but here it fails to work due to the fact that White has too little influence in the centre.

She should have increased her influence in the centre as quickly as possible by going e2-e4 now or on the next move. The game Ilincic-Hoang Thanh Trang, Budapest 2004, continued 16.♕b3 ♕d7 17.e4 b5 18.♖e1 ♗f6 19.♗f4, with chances for both sides.

16...♗f6 17.♗d2 b5 18.axb5

18...♘xb5

Far stronger was 18...axb5, intending to keep the queenside pawn front intact. After 19.b4 c4 Black would have a large strategic advantage. The covered passed pawn is strong, and Black also controls the only open file.

19.♗g2 ♗c8 20.♘e4

Now the chances are roughly equal. White is going to get the bishop pair, while Black maintains solid control in the centre.

20...♖e8 21.♘xf6+ ♕xf6 22.e4 a5 23.♖a1 ♗d7

After the dramatic first games, Anna Ushenina's seconds Alexander Khalifman and Anton Korobov seem to be at a loss what advice they should come up with.

ANASTASIYA KARLOVICH

24.♖a2 White's match problems are coming home to roost. Objectively speaking, 24.♖xa5 was White's best move, but that would make for a drawish position. Therefore, White keeps the queenside pawns on the board, but she will be unable to prevent Black from swapping them under more favourable conditions later.
24...a4 25.♖e1 h6 26.♗e3

26...a3! Taking the initiative.
27.♕d2 axb2 28.♖xb2

28...♘c3 Hou Yifan possibly had sweet memories of Game 3, in which a powerful knight on c3 helped her to victory. In this situation it would have been better to keep the knight on b5, with the option of jumping to d4. Stronger was 28...♖a4, maintaining some initiative.
29.f3 ♖a3 30.♗f2!
Now White is slightly better.
30...♘b5

31.♖eb1
In time-trouble, White allows her advantage to slip away at once. Strong was 31.f4, with the option of working with e4-e5. Remarkably enough, White never sets her central majority moving in this particular Benoni position.
31...c4!
Hou Yifan in her element. Tactical skirmishes are looming.
32.♖xb5 ♗xb5

33.♗d4?
After this error White is lost.
33.♖xb5 would not have done either in view of 33...♖a1+ 34.♗f1 ♕xf3, and the white position collapses.
With 33.♕b4! White would have just maintained the balance, e.g. 33...♖a2 34.♕xb5 ♖xe4 35.♖f1 ♖ee2 36.♕xc4 ♕b2 37.♕c8+ ♔h7 38.♕f5+, with perpetual check.
33...c3!
This pawn push is decisive.
34.♕f2 ♕g5 35.f4 ♕g4

Now 36.♖xb5 is met by the devastating 36...♕d1+ 37.♗f1 c2.
36.♖e1 ♖ea8 37.h3 ♕c8 38.e5 ♖a1 39.exd6 c2 40.♗xa1
As soon as White had played this move, her flag fell.

After this third defeat, her third consecutive loss with the white pieces, Ushenina's position became hopeless. In Game 7, she went for the Najdorf again, but this time Hou Yifan's reaction was exemplary.
    The World Champion has provided commentary on the game herself.

NOTES BY
Hou Yifan

SI 23.1 – B84
Hou Yifan
Anna Ushenina
Taizhou 2013 (7)

We played the first six games on the stage of a huge, wide hall with arbiters, teams and spectators. Then, after a free mid-autumn day, we moved to another small but 'warm' hall with only two kind arbiters. Would the new playing atmosphere bring something fresh to us? Let's start and see ☺.
1.e4 c5 2.♘f3 d6 3.d4 cxd4 4. ♘xd4 ♘f6 5.♘c3 a6 6.♗e3

6...♘bd7!? A little surprise! This move was first played by World Champion Tigran Petrosian at the 1962 Olympiad in Varna against Jesus Diez del Corral (actually, Petrosian first played 5...♘bd7 and then 6...a6). A very interesting move instead of the normal 6...e6, which appeared in our previous two games.
7.♗e2 I decided to turn to another type of position. After the continuation 7.g4 h6 8.h4 b5 9.a4 bxa4 10. f3 ♗b7 11.♖xa4 e6 12.♘b3 d5 Black was more than fine in Andriasian-Al Sayed, Dubai 2011 (the game ended in a draw).
7...e6 8.g4 h6 9.f4

9...g5!?
A typical idea in this kind of pawn structure. The main idea is to control the e5-square by means of sacrificing a pawn, which also opens two files for Black's compensation. Besides this, some other moves have also been tried, like 9...g6 or 9...b5, but neither looks as aggressive as the text.
10.f5
If White takes the pawn, 10.fxg5 hxg5 11.♗xg5, Black will have enough compensation after 11...b5 12.a3 ♗b7 with all her active and well-coordinated pieces attacking the centre.
10...♘e5 11.h3 b5 12.a3 ♕e7 13.fxe6 fxe6 14.♘f3

14...♘fd7
The game Ponomariov-Topalov, Thessaloniki Grand Prix 2013, saw 14... ♗b7 15.♘xe5 dxe5 16.♗d3 ♕c7 17. h4 ♗c5. Black got an advantage and was a pawn up, but in the end White managed to make a draw with accurate defending.

Taizhou 2013

				1	2	3	4	5	6	7		TPR
Hou Yifan	IGM	CHN	2609	1	½	1	½	½	1	1	5½	2730
Anna Ushenina	IGM	UKR	2500	0	½	0	½	½	0	0	1½	2379

15.♕d2
Maybe I should have taken on e5 first – 15.♘xe5 ♘xe5 16.♕d2 – which would force Black's knight to e5 and leave my light-squared bishop with a better position. And after this continue as in the game.
15...♘xf3+ 16.♗xf3

16...♘e5
On e5, the dark-squared bishop would be more powerful than the knight. On the one hand it defends the weakness on d6, while on the other it will help the attack on the c-file.
After 16...♗g7!? 17.0-0-0 ♗e5 the position is unclear. It looks as if the only breakthrough is still on h4, but it's not that easy to realize.
17.♗e2 ♗g7 18.0-0-0 ♘f7 19.♗d4!
Normally, when one side has weaknesses on either the light or dark squares, you should keep the bishop of that particular colour, but this is a special case. The g7-bishop is more powerful, like the parapet of a castle.

19...♗e5
A critical moment. Maybe this was the main point of Black's idea: by exchanging the bishops she wants to solve the

Chess Software from ChessOK.com

Software Series	Software Description	Price (VAT incl.)

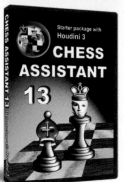

weakness on d6 and then strengthen her control of the dark squares. But Black's pieces are still undeveloped, so her plan to open more lines is a bit dubious.

But I failed to find any better solution. After 19...0-0 20.♗xg7 ♔xg7 21.♕d4+ ♕f6 22.♕b6 the dark squares are still useless to Black and the knight has to stay on f7, blocking the f-file.

And after 19...♗xd4 20.♕xd4 0-0 the aggressive break 21.e5!? tips the balance. All in all, White has comfortable play.

20.♗xe5 dxe5

21.h4!

The only way to undermine Black's control of f4. If Black doesn't take the pawn, I will just push h5, taking away the g6-square from Black, the only route for the knight to f4.

21...gxh4 22.♕e1

22...♖a7

It's difficult to suggest a good plan for Black here. According to general principles, she should try to castle and develop her pieces as soon as possible, before the position is opened. But at this point castling is not all that safe:

22...0-0 23.♖xh4 ♖d8 24.♗d3!, and White keeps one more rook on the board, which will help the attack later, after the advance g5.

23.♖xh4 ♖d7 24.♖h5

As the black king is stuck in the centre, Black cannot really connect her pieces, so maybe White should have kept the rook on the board: 24.♗d3!? ♗b7 (after 24...♕g5+ 25.♔b1 ♖g8 26.♘xb5! wins) 25.♖h5, and Black will suffer and have a tough time.

24...♖g8 25.♔b1 ♕c5 26.♖h3 ♕b6

27.♕h4?! Quite a normal move, played by hand, which just activates the queen and frees the h-rook.

But more accurate was the less conspicuous move 27.♖c1!, implementing the same idea! At the same time, the bishop stays on e2, where it will soon show its power: 27...♗b7 28.g5 hxg5 29.♕g3 ♔d8 30.♖h7, followed by ♗h5, and White is almost winning.

27...♖xd1+ 28.♘xd1 ♗b7 29.♖c3 ♕d8 30.♕f2

30...♕d4? This last mistake leads to a hopeless position.

Black cannot continue defending only with the queen.

Instead, she should have grabbed her chance to allow the knight to join the battle again!: 30...♘g5!

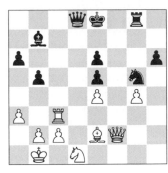

ANALYSIS DIAGRAM

31.♖d3 (31.♕a7 ♖g7! demonstrates another advantage of the knight move: it makes way for the rook: 32.♘f2 ♖f7 33.♖d3 ♕c8 with an unclear position) 31...♕c7 32.♕f6 ♗xe4 33.♖c3 ♕g7 34.♕f2 ♕b7, and basically Black will be able to hold here.

31.♕f6 ♕d6 32.♘f2

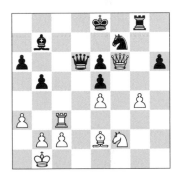

32...♔f8?! Although both sides have equal material, Black has almost run out of moves. For instance: 32...♗c6 33.g5! ♖xg5 34.♘h3, followed by ♗h5, after the rook has moved, and White is winning.

33.♖f3 ♖g7 34.♕xh6 ♔g8 35.♕f6 ♗c6 36.♖d3 ♕c5 37. g5! ♘xg5 38.♘g4 ♘f7 39.♕xe6 ♕g1+ 40.♖d1 Black resigned.

I was very glad and happy that I could participate in the Match again and regain the title. I am very grateful to FIDE, which insisted on organizing such a championship match, and to everybody all around the world who supported me ☺. ■

Undoubtedly the most common fallacy in chess is the quasi-religious belief in the primacy of openings. I was reminded of this point after following the recent Ushenina-Hou Yifan match in Taizhou, China. No one can have been surprised that the younger, more talented girl triumphed, but it was disappointing, from a gladiatorial perspective, that the defending World Champion did not put up greater fight.

In a refreshingly frank interview by Alexander Khalifman – a key member of Anna Ushenina's analytical team – the renowned St. Petersburg theoretician acknowledged that, in pre-match preparation, insufficient attention had been paid to other phases of play. Indeed, the Ukrainian could, generally speaking, be reasonably satisfied with the outcome of the introductory moves, but this did not matter a jot because she was hopelessly outclassed in the middlegame. Ushenina's woeful clock handling, in particular, caused her plenty of grief.

In some ways this was analogous to my own, solitary, World Championship experience. I was so concerned to close the yawning chasm of theoretical knowledge with Kasparov that I spent little time on anything else – importantly forgetting that my opponent could not only serve, but also volley. In fact, on only one occasion (Game 9) in twenty was I thoroughly out-prepared, but I dropped points galore elsewhere. My chronic time-trouble in the first half of the match was a consequence of immense pressure and a lack of confidence. Had I been able to cope with this better, I would have made more of the numerous opportunities I created, but then subsequently squandered. I will not make the ridiculous claim that, had I done this, the final result would have been any different, but the score, perhaps, ought to have been closer.

The opening knowledge gap between Anna Ushenina and Hou Yifan, however – if it existed at all – was relatively small. Why then did the defending champion, aided by her redoubtable seconds, fail to redress her most glaring deficiencies? I suspect the simple answer to this is that it is a lot easier to analyse specific variations than it is to contemplate, in general terms, how to deal with certain match situations which may, or may not, occur. There is also another psychological explanation for a profound opening bias: no one, at

whatever level, likes to admit that he (or she) is inept at calculation, or can't make a two-move plan. A player would rather delude himself with the thought that all will be fine if he can emerge unscathed, or perhaps even with an advantage, from this irksome initial phase – which he contemptuously dismisses as mere drudgery and memorisation (and which has, of course, nothing to do with his enormous natural talent) – into the clear, open waters of the middlegame. This is nonsense, of course, but comforting for the ego to think that way.

Actually, the idea for this article came about when someone gently requested that I write about how to form a repertoire. The preceding paragraphs are thus, in essence, a long-winded way of warning that, if you think it is your main, or indeed only problem, nine times out of ten you will be wrong. That is not to denigrate the importance of openings – merely to add a little balance. At the recent knock-out in Tromsø, Vladimir Kramnik advised Dmitry Andreikin to work hard on this area. This was not the mocking taunt of the victor to the vanquished, but a friendly bit of good advice. Looked at from another angle though, Andreikin has crossed the 2700 threshold, won the Russian Championship, reached the final of the World Cup and qualified for the Candidates' with piss-poor openings. As Vlad tacitly hints, he won't go further unless he puts in the hard yards, but the rising star hasn't exactly done badly thus far.

A few harsh and mean-spirited readers will argue that my own repertoire is so creaky and ramshackle that I am not qualified to offer advice to anyone. True, you would be better off asking Vishy Anand for tips, but as he doubtless requires greater remuneration to be induced to divulge any of his secrets, you will have to make do with me. So, here are a few droplets of wisdom, in no particular order, for the typical club or tournament player, distilled from a lengthy professional career. Nota bene: this is by no means the only way to approach things. It is an individual philosophy that has worked well enough for your writer. Incidentally, the points frequently overlap…

1 Know thyself

You may fancy yourself as a bold gambiteer, but your attacks are repulsed more often than they succeed.

Stick to your strengths. Winning is much more enjoyable than glorious failure. And, by the way, it is much easier when you sacrifice your opponent's pieces, not your own. If you don't have time, or can't be bothered, to study vast amounts of theory, don't enter cutting-edge, sharp variations or you will only be inviting disaster. Play within your limits. On the other hand, if booking up on tactical lines in, say, the Sicilian Dragon gives you a thrill, go for it. There is always the possibility you will be out-prepared by your opponent, but a bigger danger in my view for those who enjoy forcing continuations, is the tendency to ignore 'dull' or noncritical lines. Such players often drift into inferiority because they become bored and their brains switch off.

2 Computers change everything

Magnus is an extremely fine player, but your laptop is stronger. Use it. You are a fool if you don't. This goes from checking your own games immediately afterwards (e.g. discovering that 'unfamiliar' line you found yourself was first played in 1847 and has subsequently appeared in 2,348 games and that, by the way, you happened to choose the weakest continuation...) to preparing new ideas. In my more lyrical moments I have compared analysis engines to chainsaws chopping down the Amazon. While it is true that certain positions have been laid bare and turned into an arid wasteland, numerous other possibilities have opened up. Engines don't come with the same prejudices that we do and so they very often suggest totally original ideas.

3 Variety is the spice of life

The English player Michael Franklin was faithful to the London System his entire career. While there is nothing wrong with the London System (indeed, I occasionally try it myself), if you wheel it out game after game for decades on end, not only do you fail to develop as a player, chess also becomes excruciatingly tedious. And if you are not enjoying the game, you are finished as a player sooner or later. I remember Julian Hodgson once lamenting that he was unable to get an advantage (again) in his beloved Trompowsky. My fellow Bolton grandmaster David Norwood sagely commented, 'I am not a professional, but if I were, I would either fix it or learn something new.' Jules quit chess a

> 'Magnus is an extremely fine player, but your laptop is stronger. Use it. You are a fool if you don't.'

short while later. Constant repetition is not advisable even for a solid, irrefutable opening, but is plain suicide for an unsound opening. Not even club players can get away with playing, say, the Latvian Gambit on a regular basis because someone, before too long, is going to switch on that laptop and bust it easily. Sharp lines, as I have already mentioned, require constant maintenance. If you are relatively idle, swot for a specific game and then change next time. This is more or less the only way to survive when lazy. Return to the same variation only when people have forgotten that it is in your repertoire.

4 A moving target is a lot harder to hit than a stationary one

An analysis engine is like a powerful missile: if you know precisely where to aim at, it can cause terrible destruction. It is not even necessary to have a killing novelty prepared: merely knowing much more than your opponent about a specific complicated position puts you at an enormous advantage. Thus the ideal thing, from a defensive perspective, is to make yourself unpredictable by preparing vast numbers of systems and knowing them all equally well. However, if your name is not Vassily Ivanchuk, it is still safer to chop and change regularly, even at the risk of not always knowing exactly what you are doing.

5 Don't tire yourself out

This is an incredibly common mistake. If you play a closed tournament where you know your opponents in advance, it is possible, and indeed advisable, to prepare beforehand. If, like most people, you mainly participate in opens, you have little choice but leave that until prior to the game. Toleration levels vary from individual to individual, but anything more than about two hours is counter-productive for me. For double rounds, anything beyond the briefest of examinations ('ah, he is a 1.d4 player') becomes risky – even for young players. I am grateful to my 22-year-old friend Carla Heredia, who ruined her most recent event in El Salvador through overwork, for reminding me of this important fact. ∎

Başking in Siberian warmth

A Although he was eliminated in the third round of the World Cup, Pavel Eljanov left Tromsø in a good mood. The Ukrainian grandmaster hadn't lost any of his classical games, gained 10 rating points and got home in time to travel on to the 14th Anatoly Karpov tournament in Poikovsky. Basking in the warmth of the legendary Siberian hospitality, Eljanov maintained his good form, collected a further 13 rating points and had one of his finest tournament successes to date. He suffered only one defeat; against runner-up Alexander Motylev, the proud winner of the 2009 edition. The people in Poikovsky like to invite back old friends and the Russian GM has been a welcome guest ever since. Motylev had also been in Tromsø, as the second of Sergey Karjakin, who happened to be the player that knocked out Eljanov...

NOTES BY
Pavel Eljanov

NI 21.5 – E32
Pavel Eljanov
Dmitry Jakovenko
Poikovsky 2013 (5)

1.d4
When we met in the World Cup in Tromsø, it was the neighbouring pawn that went into battle against Dmitry: 1.c4. In that game I was successful and I went forward into the next round. It is said 'leave well alone', but when people devised this saying they could not have imagined that Houdini would appear ☺. The tendency is such that with careful analytical work Black can equalize practically everywhere.
The tactic of choosing an opening for a certain opponent can be called 'catwalk fashion design', as Kramnik called it in one of his interviews. But for me it more resembles the table game of *Battleships*. You have to guess in which field of knowledge and ability the opponent is most vulnerable and fire at those squares, not allow-

With 14 editions so far the Poikovsky tournament has become a solid fixture on the chess calendar. If there is one place where the players know what they can expect, it is here in Western Siberia. Anatoly Karpov will be guest of honour, there will be vodka sprinkled dinners, and on the free day the players will plant trees. Assisted by a young local expert tournament winner Pavel Eljanov planted a fir tree. The Ukrainian grandmaster played well and won deservedly. In his game notes he also reveals that he knows a thing or two about *Battleships*!

ing the opponent to draw breath and launch a counterattack.

1...♘f6 2.c4 e6 3.♘c3 ♗b4 4.♕c2 0-0 5.♘f3 c5 6.dxc5 ♘a6

7.c6!?

Morozevich's variation. It is hard to imagine that in this way White can fight for an advantage, but at least he is able to obtain an asymmetric pawn structure.

7...bxc6

When Ruslan Ponomariov encountered this variation for the first time, he tried to play symmetrically, but he was unsuccessful, to put it mildly: 7...dxc6 8.a3 ♗xc3+ 9.♕xc3 ♘c5 10. ♗e3 ♘ce4? 11.♕e5 b5? 12.g4!, with

a decisive advantage in Morozevich-Ponomariov, Moscow 2008 (1-0, 37).

8.e3!?

This move has occurred rather rarely, but it is the latest one that Morozevich has tried in this position. Here Dmitry began thinking for a long time. Continuing the analogy with *Battleships*, I correctly worked out the placing of his ships and disabled one of them! The main move is 8.a3, but it is precisely here that Black fairly quickly found a worthy antidote. This is what the 12th World Champion played in a blitz tournament: 8...♗xc3+ 9.♕xc3 ♘c5 10.♕c2 a5 11.♗e3 ♕e7 12.g3 a4 13.♗g2 ♗a6 14.♘e5 ♖fc8 15.♖d1 d5 16.0-0 ♘cd7 17.♘xd7 ♘xd7 18.♕xa4

♗xc4 with a black edge in Morozevich-Karpov, Moscow 2008 (1-0, 33).

8...d5

The latest game at high level went 8...♘c5 9.♗d2 a5 10.a3 ♗xc3 11.♗xc3 ♘ce4 12.♗xf6 ♘xf6 13.c5 a4 14.0-0-0 ♖a5 15.♔b1 ♕e7 16.♖c1 ♗a6 17. ♗xa6 ♖xa6 18.♖hd1.

ANALYSIS DIAGRAM

A strategically interesting position was reached, and in the end Morozevich was able to outplay Alekseev (Saratov 2011, 1-0, 60).

9.♗e2 ♘e4 10.0-0 ♘xc3 11.bxc3 ♗e7 12.♖b1 ♘c5 13.♗a3 ♘e4 14.♗xe7 ♕xe7 15.♗d3 ♘f6 16. ♘e5 ♕d6

For the moment Dmitry plays well – a long-range battle is in progress. Apart from a time advantage, I had not achieved any dividends.

17.f4 ♗a6 18.♕a4 ♗xc4 19. ♗xc4 dxc4 20.♕xc4 ♘d5 21. ♖fd1

21...♕a3?!

Not a mistake, but a shot that missed – Dmitry failed to hit one of my ships! Now Black has to play rather carefully. 21...f6!? 22.♘f3 ♖ab8 was quite possible. I was intending to play 23.♖b3, but after 23...♘xe3 24.♖xd6 ♘xc4 25. ♖xe6 ♖be8! the computer gives complete equality and it is right.

22.♕b3!

This pawn sacrifice – of a single-deck ship – is the only possibility of maintaining the fading initiative! After 22. ♖d3 ♖ab8 23.♖f1 ♖b2 Black launches a dangerous counterattack.

22...♕xb3 23.♖xb3 ♘xe3 24.♖d7 ♘d5 25.c4

25...♘b6!

The correct decision. 25...♘xf4 26. ♘xc6 g5 27.c5 a5 28.♘e5 looks very dangerous. For a human, playing such a position is terrifying.

26.♖c7

26...c5

In analysis immediately after the

game it appeared that 26...f6 was the simplest way of reaching the haven of a draw. But a more detailed analysis shows that Black has to play extremely accurately – in order to reach a rather unpleasant rook ending with his king cut off.

ANALYSIS DIAGRAM

A) After 27.♘xc6 Black does indeed make a draw without difficulty: 27... ♖f7 28.♖xf7 ♔xf7 29.♖b4 ♔e8 30. ♘xa7 ♖xa7 31.♖xb6 ♔d7;
B) But White has 27.♖g3! g6 28.♘xg6 hxg6 29.♖xg6+ ♔h8 30.♖h6+ ♔g8 31.♖hh7

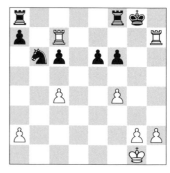

ANALYSIS DIAGRAM

and now it transpires that even with the pawn on h2 Black has problems. Strictly the only plan of defence is to double rooks on the d-file with the idea of exchanging on d7: 31...♖fd8 32. ♖cg7+ ♔f8 33.h4 ♖d1+ 34.♔h2 ♖ad8 35.♖f7+ ♔e8 36.♖e7+ ♔f8 37.c5 ♘d7 38.h5 ♖d5 39.h6 ♖h5+ 40.♔g3 ♖xh6 41.♖hf7+ ♔g8 42.♖xd7 ♖xd7 43. ♖xd7 ♖h5 44.♖xa7 ♖xc5 45.a4 and with accurate play Black can probably make a draw, but such endings with the king cut off on the back rank always harbour considerable dangers.

Poikovsky 2013																cat. XVIII
				1	2	3	4	5	6	7	8	9	10		TPR
1 Pavel Eljanov	IGM	UKR	2702	*	0	1	½	½	1	1	½	½	1	6	2809
2 Alexander Motylev	IGM	RUS	2663	1	*	½	½	½	½	½	1	½	½	5½	2768
3 Ernesto Inarkiev	IGM	RUS	2693	0	½	*	½	½	1	½	0	1	1	5	2728
4 Alexander Onischuk	IGM	USA	2667	½	½	½	*	½	0	½	½	1	½	4½	2688
5 Ian Nepomniachtchi	IGM	RUS	2723	½	½	½	½	*	½	½	0	½	1	4½	2682
6 Emil Sutovsky	IGM	ISR	2660	0	½	0	1	½	*	½	1	1	0	4½	2689
7 Dmitry Jakovenko	IGM	RUS	2724	0	½	½	½	½	½	*	1	½	½	4½	2682
8 Viktor Bologan	IGM	MDA	2672	½	0	1	½	1	0	0	*	0	1	4	2644
9 Viktor Laznicka	IGM	CZE	2677	½	½	0	0	½	0	½	1	*	½	3½	2607
10 Ivan Cheparinov	IGM	BUL	2678	0	½	0	½	0	1	½	0	½	*	3	2562

27.h4!! Again the only way of maintaining the intrigue is to launch a dangerous torpedo along the h-file.

27...g6? Missed! And this is the decisive error. Also bad was 27...f6 28. ♖g3 g6 29.♘xg6 hxg6 30.♖xg6+ ♔h8

Poikovsky's Class of 2013: Ian Nepomniachtchi, Viktor Laznicka, Emil Sutovsky, Alexander Onischuk, chief arbiter Yuri Lobanov, Alexander Motylev, Pavel Eljanov, Ivan Cheparinov, Dmitry Jakovenko, Ernesto Inarkiev and Victor Bologan.

ANALYSIS DIAGRAM

31.♖h6+ ♔g8 32.♖hh7 ♖fd8 33. ♖cg7+ ♔f8 34.h5 and Black is lost. And 27...h6 28.h5 ♘c8 29.♖b5 ♘d6 30. ♖bxc5 is also clearly better for White. The only chance of remaining afloat was 27...h5! with the idea of nevertheless playing 28...f6. Now White has to make some useful move, but in transpires that on the threshold of forcing play it is not easy for him to strengthen his position.

ANALYSIS DIAGRAM

A) At first sight the most logical is 28.♔f2, but in some variations the king comes under fire here: 28...f6 29. ♖g3 g5 30.♘d3 g4 31.♖xc5 f5 32.♖e3 ♖fd8. Black is threatening in various ways to play his knight to e4 with gain of tempo, and it is hard for White to strengthen his position: 33.♔e2 ♘a4, with counterplay;

B) 28.♔h2 f6 29.♖g3 g5 30.♘d3. Now Black can give up his pawn on g5, retaining good drawing chances. But it is simpler and 'more human' to block the kingside: 30...g4 31.♖xc5 f5 32.♖e3:

ANALYSIS DIAGRAM

B1) Not all the problems are solved by 32...♖ac8 33.♖xc8 ♖xc8 34.c5 ♘d7 35.♖xe6 ♘xc5 36.♘xc5 ♖xc5 37.♖h6 ♖c4 38.♖xh5 ♖xf4 39.♔g3 ♖f1 40. ♖h6 f4+ 41.♔xg4 ♖f2 42.a4 ♖xg2+ 43.♔xf4. This looks like a theoreti-

cal draw, but it is not so clear how to reduce it to the Vancura position;

B2) But after the accurate 32... ♖fd8!, it would appear that Black can hold the position: 33.♖c7 ♖d4 34.♘c5 ♖xc4 35.♘xe6 ♖xc7 36.♘xc7 ♖c8.

28.h5 Now my torpedo inflicts decisive damage!

28...f6 A further mistake, but it is already hard to offer Black any good advice. After 28...♖ad8 29.h6 ♖d4 30. ♖xa7 ♘xc4 31.♘d7 White is winning. Possibly the lesser evil was 28...♖fc8 29.♖xf7 ♖f8 30.hxg6 hxg6 31.♖b7 ♖fb8 32.♖xb8+ ♖xb8 33.a4, but all the black pawns are so weak that the position is a technical loss.

29.♘g4! The killer.

29...g5 30.fxg5 fxg5 31.♘h6+ ♔h8 32.♘f7+ ♔g8 33.♘xg5 h6 34.♘h7 ♖f5 35.♖g3+ ♔h8 36. ♖g6 Black resigned.

NOTES BY
Alexander Motylev

RL 13.5 – C84
Alexander Motylev
Pavel Eljanov
Poikovsky 2013 (6)

1.e4 e5 2.♘f3 ♘c6 3.♗b5 a6
Pavel surprised me slightly by avoiding the Caro-Kann Defence, which in recent times has become his main opening. **4.♗a4 ♘f6 5.0-0 ♗e7 6. d3 b5 7.♗b3 d6 8.a3** A currently fashionable system, promising White at least some play in relatively fresh positions.

8...♗g4!? A surprise! It would appear that this is a novelty, prepared at home. On encountering this unexpected reply, I made several natural moves.
9.♗e3! I think that this is the strongest continuation.
9...d5! This is Black's idea. In the event of 9...0-0 10.♘c3 the game would have reverted to main theory lines.
10.h3 It is useful to drive back the bishop.
10...♗h5 11.♘bd2 0-0 12.♖e1
Despite the opening surprise, on the whole I was more or less happy with my position, whereas Pasha, by contrast, sank into thought. Black faces a wide choice of possibilities.
12...d4?! I think that this decision to simplify the position is the initial cause of Black's subsequent difficulties. He should have maintained the tension in the centre by 12...♖b8 or 12...♖e8.

13.♗g5 h6
Black would have been happy to exchange the dark-squared bishops by 13...♘d7, but White has a tactical refutation – 14.♗d5 ♗xg5 15.♗xc6 ♗xd2 16.♕xd2 ♖b8 (16...♗xf3 17. ♗xa8 ♗xg2 18.♔xg2 ♕xa8 is better) 17.g4, winning a pawn.
14.♗xf6 ♗xf6 15.♗d5!

15...♕e8?! This is over-subtle.
15...♕d7? was bad because of 16. ♘xe5! ♕xd5 17.exd5 ♗xd1 18.♘xc6 ♗xc2 19.♘b4.
Both of us disliked 15...♕d6 because of 16.a4, after which Black is forced to spoil his pawn structure on the queenside. But it would appear that this was not so terrible. The computer points out that White gains an advantage with the subtle 16.♖c1! (here 16.♗xc6? is not dangerous for Black, since he can interpose 16...♗xf3!) 16... ♖ac8 17.♗xc6! ♗xf3 (17...♕xc6? 18. ♘xe5!) 18.♗xf3 ♕xc6 19.c3 dxc3 20. ♖xc3 ♕d7 21.♕c2.
16.♗xc6!? After spending more than half an hour on calculations, I decided that this forcing combination leads to an advantage for White.
Little was promised by 16.a4 ♖b8, but the subtle 16.♖c1 was possible, when White gains an advantage as in the 15...♕d6 16.♖c1! variation.
16...♕xc6
In the event of 16...♗xf3? Black simply loses a pawn after 17.♗xe8 ♗xd1 18.♗xf7+.
17.♘xe5 ♗xe5
17...♗xd1? was bad in view of 18. ♘xc6 ♗xc2 19.♘b4 ♗a4 20.♘d5 (or 20.e5).
18.♕xh5 ♕xc2 19.♘f3!

19...f6!
The only way! Any bishop move would have led to a big advantage for White: 19...♗f6 20.e5 ♗g5 21.h4 ♗e7 22.♘xd4 ♕xd3 23.♘f5 or 19...♗f4 20.♕g4 ♗g5 21.h4 ♗e7 22.♘xd4 ♕xb2 23.♘f5.
Initially I came to a halt at this position in my calculations before the 16th move, not seeing any way to gain an advantage, but then I found the game continuation and I realized that White's attack on the light squares would be very dangerous.
20.♘h4!
White leaves his queenside pawns to be taken by the enemy queen, but in return he develops a very strong initiative on the kingside.

20...c5?
Black overlooks the opponent's reply. The computer gives 20...♗f7!! as the only move, but here also, after 21.♕g4!? (another way of developing the attack is also very dangerous – 21. ♘f5!? ♕xd3 22.♖ad1 ♕b3 23.♕g4 ♔h8 24.f4 ♗d6 25.e5) 21...♕xb2 22. f4 ♗d6 23.♖f1 White's attack, following the same pattern as in the game, is very dangerous.
21.f4! ♗c7

The pawn cannot be captured in view of the loss of the bishop after 21...♗xf4 22.♕d5+ ♔h7 (22...♔h8 23.♘g6+) 23.♕f5+.

22.♘f5! An important move. White had many tempting continuations, but this is the strongest.

22...♖f7 Here also the pawn cannot be captured – 22...♗xf4 23.♘e7+ ♔h7 24.♕f5+.

23.♖f1!? 23.e5! fxe5 24.♕g6! was stronger, forcing Black to give up the exchange by 24...♖xf5 25.♕xf5, with a technically won position.

The immediate 23.♕g6? would have been a blunder in view of 23...♗xf4! 24.g3 ♗d2!.

23...♖af8 White would also have won in the event of 23...♕b3 24.♕g6 ♔h8 25.♖ac1!? ♗b6 26.e5!.

24.♖f3?!

Careless. It was more accurate not to allow the king to go to h7 – 24.♕g6 ♔h8 25.♖f3.

24...♔h7

24...♕b3 25.♖af1.

25.♖af1

I thought that this position was easily won, but Black has a way of hindering the development of the attack.

25...♕d2? 25...♕e2! was the only move that did not allow White to win quickly: 26.♕h4 (after 26.♘h4!? c4! 27.♘g6 f5 White undoubtedly has the advantage, but the battle continues) 26...c4 27.♖g3

ANALYSIS DIAGRAM

27...h5!!. It is surprising that here White does not win immediately, but apparently he wins rather more slowly after 28.♖gf3 g6 29.♘g3.

26.e5! After this breakthrough there is no defence.

26...♗xe5

26...fxe5 leads to mate: 27.♖g3 exf4 28.♖xg7+! ♖xg7 29.♕xh6+ ♔g8 30.♕xg7 mate. If 26...♕e2 an elegant diverting move decides matters – 27.e6! ♕xe6 28.♖g3 ♖g8 29.♖g6 ♔h8

30.♘xh6 gxh6 31.♖xh6+ ♔g7 32.♖g6+ ♔f8 33.♕h6+ ♖gg7 (33...♖fg7 34.♖xf6+) 34.♕h8+ and wins.

27.♖3f2! This is more accurate than 27.fxe5 g6 28.♕g4 gxf5 29.♕xf5+ ♔h8 30.exf6 ♕g5, although even here after 31.♕e6! White should win without difficulty.

27...♕xd3 28.fxe5 fxe5

29.♖f3! Avoiding a devilish trap – 29.♘xh6?? ♕xf1+!!, when the advantage is now with Black.

29...♕d2

29...♖xf5 loses to 30.♖xf5 g6 31.♖f7+ ♖xf7 32.♖xf7+ ♔g8 33.♕f3!. After 29...♕c4 the sacrifice 30.♘xh6! now works, since the rook on f3 is defended: 30...♕xf1+ 31.♔xf1 ♖xf3+ 32.gxf3 gxh6 33.♔e2 and wins.

30.♘xh6! ♖xf3 31.♘f7+!

This is more accurate than 31.♘f5+ ♕h6 32.♕xf3, although here, too, White wins without any particular problems.

31...♕h6 32.♕xf3

Black resigned, since the endgame after 32...♕e3+ (32...♕g6 33.♘g5+!) 33.♕xe3 dxe3 is completely hopeless – 34.♘g5+ ♔g8 35.♖xf8+ ♔xf8 36.♘e6+ ♔e7 37.♘xc5. ■

A

Casting the dice in Paris

After the previous Grand Prix tournament in Beijing (see New In Chess 2013/6) Veselin Topalov and Shakhriyar Mamedyarov emerged at the top of the overall standings. While Topalov secured his spot in the Candidates' by becoming overall Grand Prix winner, Mamedyarov still had to wait for the event in Paris to unfold. The only two players who could still challenge Mamedyarov, who didn't play in the final leg himself, were Fabiano Caruana and Alexander Grischuk. Since they both had to win the event outright (even sharing first wouldn't do), the chances of that happening didn't seem too high to me. Yet, running ahead a bit, I can tell you that even though it indeed didn't happen, the scenario of the tournament left Spielberg and Tarantino green with envy.

For this time I will have mercy on you, dear reader, and will not delve into my own adventures, as yours truly played one of his worst tournaments ever and scored a grey -4, while probably burning 11 novelties in 12 games and not having a single bad position. The only thing that seemed funny to me in the big tournament table inside the playing hall was my own score – the draws were for some reason marked as 'X'

While the current World Championship cycle is about to come to its end with the approaching Anand-Carlsen match as its culmination, a fair number of chess professionals is already preoccupied with the next Candidates' tournament, which is to be held in March 2014. With six out of eight players already known, it was the Paris Grand Prix that was to solve the mystery of one of the last two places. **Anish Giri** was on the spot and saw how the mystery was unravelled.

and losses, as always, as 'O', which meant that in the end my tournament score ended up being something like XOXOXO (for those who don't follow all the latest smiley trends, that stands for hugs and kisses amongst young Dutch teenagers). Talking about novelties, the only other player who seemed to be quite well prepared was Fabiano Caru-

If you're so close, you have to visit Versailles! And six of the participants indeed joined the excursion on the first free day.

ana. And since, quite unlike me, Fabiano kept a cool head and also managed to play some good moves of his own, he quickly established himself at the top of the standings.

Unfortunately for Fabiano, he was not the only one who enjoyed the sweet taste of victory, and from the very first round it was Boris Gelfand who made a statement by winning his

game against no one else than yours truly. Frankly, this was a disappointing game for me. I had managed to out-prepare Boris, who repeated the variation he played in the tiebreak of his match against Anand, and unlike in some of my subsequent games I also managed to play the middle-game very well, causing Boris problems even though I had the black pieces. However, at some point I was a little too soft and then again too soft and then once more, and suddenly, after the time-trouble, I found myself in a lost position. While for me this was the beginning of the end, Boris didn't stop and won good games with white against Dominguez and Grischuk. Towards the end of the tournament he was on the beautiful score of +3 (there was more to it than that, but everything in due time). While Fabiano was getting closer and closer to his target (after Fressinet there followed Ivanchuk, another top player who got smashed without any questions or answers), the other man to watch, Alexander Grischuk, was nowhere near qualifying. Starting with −1, Alexander failed to convert his advantage in his direct encounter with Fabiano, and even though he came back in a nice game against Ivanchuk, beating the genius with the black pieces, he never crossed the 50 per cent bar. Alexander did try to go all out with black in his game against Boris Gelfand, but it was not meant to be and Boris played another great game with the white pieces. Grischuk did win his game against me, but as you can guess, that was neither a big achievement, nor did it get Alexander any closer to where he needed to be.

As Boris and Fabiano were racing to the finish line, there suddenly appeared another man with his own ambitions: Hikaru Nakamura. Hikaru, an incredibly strong player no doubt, definitely had no reason to complain about his luck, getting one free point after the other. One such 'gift' came from Fabiano, and most likely that's where the fate of the young Italian was decided.

NOTES BY
Anish Giri

GI 1.1 – D70
Hikaru Nakamura
Fabiano Caruana
Paris 2013 (7)

1.d4 ♘f6 2.c4 g6 3.f3
A topical line, which Fabiano had to face on numerous occasions, and, by the way, yours truly also had some interesting games with it.
3...d5 The principled Grünfeld way.
4.cxd5 ♘xd5

5.e4 The point is obviously that Black cannot now take the knight on c3.
For those who like weird opening ideas, I would also recommend one of Grischuk's latest tries: 1.d4 ♘f6 2.c4 g6 3.♘f3 ♗g7 4.e3!? 0-0 5.♗e2

ANALYSIS DIAGRAM

with the same point that after 5...d5 6.cxd5 ♘xd5 7.e4! Black cannot take on c3 and damage White's pawn structure, so the loss of a tempo on e2-e3-e4 justifies itself. When facing this idea by the way, Fabiano opted for a King's Indian set-up, which is quite logical.

5...♘b6 6.♘c3 ♗g7 7.♗e3
Now Black has quite some choices, but Fabiano's in this game seems to be the most reliable one, according to the latest top-level games.

7...0-0 8.♕d2 ♘c6 Once Fabiano mixed up the move order in this position and played 8...♕d6?! at once.

'Fabiano engaged in a 50-minute think. According to some inside information, he was digesting a 300-gram red steak.'

Perhaps this could serve as a warning? But who am I to say that, since I myself mix up move orders on a daily basis?
9.0-0-0 ♕d6 10.h4

Not the most common, but obviously the most straightforward way to try and punish Black for his dubious-looking set-up. Normally, though, he shouldn't be punished that easily.
10...♖d8 11.♘b5 ♕d7 12.h5 a6 13.♘c3

13...♘xd4
13...♗xd4 is also possible and here, too, Black has to recapture with the f-pawn after 14.hxg6. That's why it's even harder to understand what Fabiano had mixed up. From my personal experience I can tell that very peculiar thoughts can get inside a chess player's mind sometimes.
14.hxg6 Here Fabiano engaged in a 50-minute think. According to some inside information, he was digesting a 300-gram red steak. I heard this had worked well for a great player of the past, but everyone is different. According to the same insider, the next day Caruana took fish, the phosphoros worked immediately and Fabiano went on to win a brilliant game against the leader, Boris Gelfand.

14...hxg6?? Inexplicable, as this move is not only dangerous, but also loses by force.

An inexplicable mistake in his game against Nakamura cost Fabiano Caruana dearly. He fought on admirably but in the end shared first place was not enough to qualify for the Candidates' tournament.

15.♗xd4 Also quite strong is 15.♕f2-h4, but it's safer to win a queen.

15...♕xd4 15...♗xd4 is hopeless too: 16.♕h6 ♕d6 17.♕h7+ ♔f8 18.♖xd4! ♕xd4 19.♕h8+ ♕xh8 20. ♖xh8+ ♔g7 21.♗xd8.

16.♕e1

And Black loses material. He kept on fighting, but the game is basically over here. **16...♕xd1+ 17.♘xd1 ♘a4 18.b3 ♘c5 19.e5 ♗f5 20.f4 a5 21.♘f3 a4 22.b4 ♘b3+ 23. axb3 a3 24.♘c3 e6 25.♘e3 a2 26.♕a1 ♗f8 27.♘xf5 gxf5 28.b5 c6 29.bxc6 ♖dc8 30.♗c4 ♖xc6 31.♘d4 ♖cc8 32.♔c2 ♗b4 33.g4 fxg4 34.f5** Black resigned.

One of Fabiano Caruana's strengths is his unshakable self-confidence and his ability to take each game on its own merit. In fact, he immediately bounced back to the top of the standings by beating the leader in their head-to-head encounter. Another impressive one.

SI 31.5 – B30
Fabiano Caruana
Boris Gelfand
Paris 2013 (8)

1.e4 c5 2.♘f3 ♘c6
I think I finally understood why Boris keeps playing the Sveshnikov Variation and keeps suffering in the Rossolimo, game after game. The idea is to confuse his colleagues and at important moments to strike and win brilliant games in the Najdorf, where Black has a much happier life.

3.♗b5
These days this is very much the main line at top level. Even after all the efforts by Gelfand and Radjabov, who keep fighting against it as Black, the Rossolimo is still alive and kicking. Kicking, in fact, like never before.

3...e6 It's purely by chance, I think, that this move is much more popular than 3...d6 or 3...g6. Fashion follows the World Championship match.

4.0-0
4.♗xc6 bxc6 was played in the Anand-Gelfand match in Moscow 2012, but I think it went out of fashion once the invincible Magnus almost got mated with the white pieces against Radjabov.

4...♘ge7

5.d4!? An old move, which I had been planning to (re)introduce at top level for quite a while. But this time Fabiano got the first chance.
5.♖e1 a6 6.♗f1 caused quite some headaches to the Gelfand/Radjabov duo, but I guess that by now Boris can tell you the forced draw here even if you wake him up in the middle of the night.

5...cxd4 6.♘xd4 ♕b6
6...♘g6 or 6...♘xd4 also seem logical. Practice will tell what's the best way to proceed.

7.♘xc6

7...bxc6
There are three other possible captures, all of which make some sense.

Again, what is the best way for Black remains to be seen. However, one thing is clear: Black should definitely deviate from this game at some point.
8.♗d3 ♘g6

9.c4
If I remember correctly, I wanted to get the same set-up as Fabiano, but with my bishop on e2. The difference is not immediately obvious to me, but the plan is the same: finish my development and play against the knight on g6.
9...♗e7 10.♘c3 0-0

11.♖b1!
Preparing the development of the c1-bishop, with b2-b4 coming to mind later.
11...♕c7 12.♗e3

12...e5?!
Here 12...♘f4!? was suggested as an improvement: 13.♗c2, and only now 13...e5 14.g3 (14.b4!?) 14...♘e6, and the knight is very much in the game. This definitely makes a lot of sense, and Fabiano would have to come up with something really clever in order to prove his advantage. Here the position is unclear, e.g. 15.f4 ♖b8 16.f5

'Ruslan Ponomariov deserved to win a game or two, standing up for all of us and daring to mention to the guide that he might have a slight French accent.'

♘d4! 17.♗xd4 exd4 18.♕xd4 ♗f6, and Black has compensation for the pawn, thanks to his dark squares.
13.g3!
Cutting off the knight, as promised. 13.c5 ♘f4 14.♗c4 also looks nice, but Fabiano played more conceptually.
13...d6
This allows 14.b4, but c4-c5 was a threat as well.

14.b4!

Now Black has two problems. One is his knight on g6, the other is his d5-square, which will soon be in full ownership of the c3-knight, after an eventual b5-push.
14...♗e6 15.♕d2 ♖ac8
15...a6 doesn't change the situation long-term after 16.a4, with the eventual b4-b5 break coming anyway.
16.b5 Black's position is pretty hopeless, and in fact I was even surprised how much resistance Gelfand still managed to put up in this game. On top of all his problems, the a7-pawn will also be lost soon.

16...♗d8 17.♖fc1 ♕d7 18.bxc6 ♖xc6 19.♘d5

19...♗b6
Giving up a pawn in order to exchange some pieces. But as the old Chinese proverb goes: a pawn is still a pawn.
19...f5 doesn't change much. After 20.exf5 ♗xf5 21.♕c2 White is in full control and Black has no counterplay whatsoever.
20.♘xb6 axb6 21.♗xb6 ♖a8
Black cannot do much, so Boris tries to regroup his pieces. **22.♗f1 ♕c8 23.♖b4 ♘f8 24.a4 ♘d7 25.a5 h6 26.h4 ♔h7 27.♕e3 ♘c5**

28.f4!
White is ready to open another front.
28...exf4 29.gxf4 f5 30.exf5 ♗xf5
Black isn't losing by force yet, but
White is fully in charge.
31.♖e1
31.♗g2?? runs into 31...♘d3!.
31...d5 Desperation, but with all his
pieces being so powerful the white
king can easily survive one check.

**32.cxd5 ♖g6+ 33.♔f2 ♘d7 34.h5
♖g4 35.♗h3 ♘f6 36.♕c1 ♕f8 37.
♖c4 ♕f7 38.♗xg4** Black dominates
the light squares on the kingside and
the white king is quite open, but unfortunately for Black, he lacks a piece
or two for a proper attack.
38...♘xg4+ 39.♔g1 ♕xh5

**40.♕d2 ♕h4 41.♖e2 ♖f8 42.♖c3
♕h5 43.d6 ♖f6 44.d7 ♖g6 45.
♖g2**
Black can no longer create the threat
of a check, so Boris resigned. A flawless game by Fabiano!

With Hikaru Nakamura yet again getting lucky against Ivanchuk (it's nothing personal, just facts), Fabiano was
still half a step behind the American. Not only did Nakamura survive
a terrible middlegame, he even managed to get a full point (Ivanchuk
lost on time in an equal position).
The next game, played after the second rest day...

Hang on, rest day... Let's get back
in time a little. After four rounds we
had the first rest day. Since we were
staying in Versailles, right next to the
Château... Château, not Palace, as we
were informed by the guide ('Palace
iz inside of ze cíty, while Château iz
outside of ze cíty! Do u undestand'?'),

**Anish Giri and Ruslan Ponomariov,
who believes that a French accent
is good for the atmosphere.**

most of the players joined the marvel-
lously guided excursion to the Château, and even the most aggressive
and uncompromising chess fighters
couldn't suppress a smile when the
entertaining French guide with his
encyclopaedic knowledge of French
history was telling a story or two
about the French 'no-bi-li-ty'. By the
way, I do think that Ruslan Ponomariov deserved to win a game or two,
standing up for all of us and daring
to mention to the guide that he might
have a slight French accent ('but it's
good for the atmosphere,' as the ex-
World Champion pointed out). But,
as you will see, the rough world of
professional chess is full of pain and
injustice.

Now back to the second rest day.
I don't know how the other players spent it, as nothing was organized for us. All I know is that my second, hard-working young Dutch GM
Robin van Kampen (even after –4 still
my friend), spent a couple of hours
looking at the Blumenfeld Gambit.
According to him, this would be the
choice of Fabiano Caruana, who was
in a must-win situation against your
young storyteller. Fortunately for
me, Fabiano didn't have such a creative second with him and ended up
playing some dull modern-mod-
ern Benoni. The position was quite
unbalanced for most of the game,
but at some point Fabiano suddenly
got real winning chances. In time-
trouble Fabiano first made a terrible blunder, but when I suddenly got
very optimistic, he managed to pull
himself together and found a strong
defence. After the time-control the
game should have ended in a draw
quickly, but as if obeying the tournament standings, Fabiano ended up
on the pushing side anyway. Still, my
position was quite tenable, and even
though I did have a nervous moment
or two in time-trouble, I managed to
defend quite easily. So Fabiano faced
the hard task of overtaking the leader,
who by this time was still half a point
ahead.

Although Hikaru Nakamura did get lucky against Ponomariov at one point in their game, somehow they both failed to notice that two moves later it was he who missed a chance to virtually secure first place.

NI 23.8 – E37
Hikaru Nakamura
Ruslan Ponomariov
Paris 2013 (9)

1.d4 ♘f6 2.c4 e6 3.♘c3 ♗b4 4.♕c2 d5 5.a3 ♗xc3+ 6.♕xc3 c5 7.dxc5 ♘e4 8.♕c2 ♘c6 9.e3 ♕a5+ 10.♗d2 ♘xd2 11.♕xd2 dxc4 12.♕xa5 ♘xa5 13.♖c1 b5 14.cxb6 ♗b7 15.♘f3 ♔e7 So far all of this has been played before, but here Nakamura suddenly goes wrong:

16.♘d2?

Instead, 16.bxa7 ♗xf3 17.gxf3 ♖xa7 is known to be a forced draw. Black is too active, and even though the c4-pawn will fall, he will eventually pick up both the b2- and a3-pawns.
16...axb6 17.♗xc4

17...♖hd8?
A very bad move after a long think. This is just too clever.

17...♖ac8 looks just too natural. So natural that I cannot even give it an exclamation mark. White is clearly worse here:

ANALYSIS DIAGRAM

A) 18.0-0 ♖hd8 19.b4 was what I thought was Hikaru's idea during the game. In fact, White is in danger even after the simple 19...♖xd2+ 20.bxa5 bxa5, as his a-pawn can prove to be vulnerable;

B) 18.♔e2!? ♖xc4! (capturing with the knight is merely a draw. Here Black is winning material) 19.♘xc4 ♗a6 20.b4 ♘xc4 21.a4, with some drawing chances for White: 21...b5!? 22.a5 ♔d6. Black will regroup his bishop to c6 and push some pawns on the kingside. Objectively, though, I do think that White should be able to hold this, thanks to his passed pawn. But who am I to judge?

C) 18.♔d1? was proposed by a friend of mine and caused me some problems blindfolded, but the computer points out a nice finesse: 18...♖hd8 19.♗a2 ♗xg2 20.♖xc8

ANALYSIS DIAGRAM

20...♗f3+!! 21.♔e1 ♖xc8, and Black wins material.

18.♗b5! Strong, but apparently the players didn't even realize how strong this move is.
18...♖ac8 19.♖c3?
Hikaru was probably in saving mode after he had seen 18...♖ac8 and was happy to escape. In fact, he didn't need to escape, as he can remain a pawn up after the simple but quite hidden resource 19.♖xc8 ♖xc8

ANALYSIS DIAGRAM

20.♔d1!!. The king protects all the penetration squares, all by itself. Black is just a pawn down, as any attempt to generate counterplay fails, e.g. 20...♗xg2?! 21.♖g1 ♗h3?! 22.♖xg7 ♗f5 23.♖g3 ♖c2? 24.b4! ♘b7 25.e4!, and White wins. Instead, Black should play 20...f5, and then push all the other pawns on the kingside in hopes of counterplay, but that's pretty sad.
19...♖xc3 20.bxc3
Draw.

With two rounds to go, it was between Nakamura, Gelfand and Caruana, with the former two playing each other in the penultimate round. In a very must-win situation, Fabiano did win his game quite easily, beating the unbeatable Tomashevsky, but the game of the day definitely was the fight between the other two leaders.

SI 14.7 – B90
Hikaru Nakamura
Boris Gelfand
Paris 2013 (10)

1.e4 c5 2.♘f3 d6 3.d4 cxd4 4.♘xd4 ♘f6 5.♘c3 a6

				1	2	3	4	5	6	7	8	9	10	11	12		TPR
1	Fabiano Caruana	IGM ITA	2779	*	1	0	½	½	½	½	½	1	1	1	½	7	2844
2	Boris Gelfand	IGM ISR	2764	0	*	1	½	1	1	½	½	½	½	½	1	7	2846
3	Hikaru Nakamura	IGM USA	2772	1	0	*	1	½	½	½	½	½	1	½	½	6½	2808
4	Etienne Bacrot	IGM FRA	2723	½	½	0	*	½	½	½	1	½	½	1	1	6½	2813
5	Alexander Grischuk	IGM RUS	2785	½	0	½	½	*	½	½	½	½	1	0	1	5½	2742
6	Leinier Dominguez	IGM CUB	2757	½	0	½	½	½	*	½	½	½	½	½	1	5½	2744
7	Wang Hao	IGM CHN	2736	½	½	½	½	½	½	*	½	½	0	½	½	5	2710
8	Ruslan Ponomariov	IGM UKR	2756	½	½	½	0	½	½	½	*	½	½	½	½	5	2709
9	Evgeny Tomashevsky	IGM RUS	2703	0	½	½	½	½	½	½	½	*	½	½	½	5	2713
10	Vassily Ivanchuk	IGM UKR	2731	0	½	0	½	0	½	1	½	½	*	1	½	5	2711
11	Laurent Fressinet	IGM FRA	2708	0	½	½	0	1	½	½	½	½	0	*	½	4½	2684
12	Anish Giri	IGM NED	2737	½	0	½	0	0	0	½	½	½	½	½	*	3½	2613

cat. XX

18...0-0!

I don't know whether this can be called a novelty here, but I myself had already known for a couple of years that Black is doing well in the complications after 18...0-0. The solid 18...♖g8, which the engines prefer, is much less fun.

19.h4 g4!

20.♕f2

This move seems very dubious to me. The knight on c3 needs some extra protection and the queen on f2 doesn't contribute to that.

The most obvious reaction is 20.f4. Now it is more or less forced: 20...♘c4 21.♗xc4 ♗xd4! 22.♕xd4 ♖xc4 23.♕e3

The Najdorf Variation seems to be serving Gelfand very well of late. Apart from the fact that Boris is well aware of the latest theoretical developments and has a good feeling for this opening, he has also only been using it as a surprise weapon lately, and that, I think, explains his great score with it.

6.♗e3 ♘g4 7.♗c1 ♘f6 8.♗e3 ♘g4

13.f3

Some time ago, 13.♘f5 led to a heated discussion, which seems to have cooled down after the game Karjakin-Grischuk, Tal Memorial 2010, which ended in a forced perpetual some 30 moves later.

13...♘bc6 14.♗f2 ♗e6

14...♘g6 is the Grischuk way.

15.♕d2 ♖c8 16.0-0-0 ♘xd4 17. ♗xd4 ♕a5

18.a3

Instead, 18.♕f2 ♖c6 19.g3 0-0 20.f4 ♘d7 was played in Karjakin-Gelfand, 2012. Guess who won that one? 0-1!

9.♗g5 h6 10.♗h4 g5 11.♗g3 ♗g7 12.h3 ♘e5

Hikaru himself has been preferring 12...♘f6 recently. Theoretically speaking, both moves seem pretty decent, but 12...♘e5 is certainly the most popular. It's also a pet-line of Grischuk's.

ANALYSIS DIAGRAM

and here Black has a few ideas to get excellent play, the most typical being: 23...♖fc8! 24.f5 ♖xc3!, and the complications lead to an equal game.

20.♕e3 can also be investigated, but it seems that Black gets excellent play here, too, with the simple 20... ♘c4 21.♗xc4 ♖xc4, and the pressure along the c-file seems to be a serious argument.

20...♖c6! This move is easy to miss during analysis, as the idea of the subsequent piece sacrifice is not that obvious to everyone.

20...♘c4 is quite primitive, but here perhaps Hikaru wouldn't mind the queen being on f2, as he can play 21. ♗xg7 ♔xg7 22.♘d5!?, although here, too, I guess Black should be fine after 22...♗xd5 23.♖xd5 ♕b6!.

21.f4 ♖fc8

22.♕g3 Here 22.f5 is best. The attack on the knight on e5 was an illusion and the pawn (as well as Hikaru) should have moved on. Now Black can start complications or play more positionally: 22...♗c4 23.♗xc4 ♘xc4 (23...♖xc4?? 24.♗b6!) 24.♗xg7 ♔xg7 25.f6+ ♔g8! 26.♘d5 ♘xa3.

ANALYSIS DIAGRAM

And somehow this ends in a perpetual: 27.bxa3 ♕xa3+ 28.♔b1 ♖xc2 29.♕xc2 ♖xc2 30.♘xe7+ ♔h7 31.♖xc2 ♕a2+ 32.♔d3 ♕b3+ 33.♔d2 ♕b2+.

Finally, 22.fxe5 dxe5 is a disaster for White: 23.♗e3 ♖xc3! 24.bxc3 ♕xa3+ 25.♔d2 ♕xc3+ 26.♔e2 ♗c4+, and Black even wins.

22...♘d7

The most forcing and quite strong. 22...h5!? looked very beautiful, and I believe Black must be doing very well here, too. His g4-pawn gets extra protection and in some lines after fxe5 the bishop can give a nasty check from h6: 23.♔b1 (23.fxe5 dxe5 24.♗f2 ♗h6+!? 25.♔b1 ♖xc3) 23...♘d7!.

23.♗xg7 ♔xg7

24.f5

White can't really defend anymore, so Hikaru goes for complications.

24...♖xc3?!

This complicates matters, although Black does have a few good options here.

Best was 24...♘e5!, which wins outright: 25.fxe6 ♖xc3 26.bxc3 ♖xc3! 27. ♗d3 ♖xa3!.

25.bxc3

25...♕xa3+?!

Again 25...♘e5! was good: 26.♔d2 ♗d7, and this is a positional disaster for White.

26.♔d2 ♘f6 27.♕d3

27...♗c4

Very solid play, but slowly Hikaru is getting a chance to escape.

An interesting possibility was 27... ♘xe4+!?. Black is a rook down, but most likely he will win the queen at some point: 28.♕xe4 ♕xc3+, and now:

ANALYSIS DIAGRAM

A) 29.♔e2 ♖c4 30.♕d3 ♕e5+ 31.♔f2 ♖f4+ 32.♔g1 ♗xf5 33.♕d2 ♕c5+ 34.♔h2 g3+! 35.♔xg3 ♖g4+ 36.♔f3 e5!, and the king hunt will soon be finished. Black wins;

B) 29.♔c1 ♕a1+ 30.♔d2 ♕a5+ 31.♔e2 ♖c4 32.♖d4 ♗xf5 33.♖xc4 ♗xe4 34.♖xe4 ♔f8, and Black has many pawns, while White doesn't seem to be in time to coordinate his pieces – although this position doesn't look that obvious to me at the first sight.

28.♕d4 d5 29.exd5 ♗xd5 30. ♖g1!

Preparing ♗d3.

ALINA L'AMI

And once again the amazing Boris Gelfand showed that his second youth is far from over.

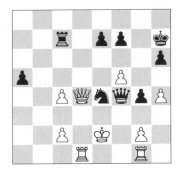

30...♕a5?! 30...♗e4! looks strong, simply attacking the pawn on f5: 31. ♗d3 ♖xd3 32.cxd3 ♕b2+ 33.♔e3 ♖xc3 and this is better for Black, even though White may win the queen with 34.♖b1 ♕c2 35.♖bc1 ♕xc1+ 36. ♖xc1 ♖xc1. Most likely Black will win this endgame, slowly but surely, as the commentator of the tournament (my double compatriot, as he nicely puts it), Sergey Tiviakov, would say.
31.♗d3 ♗e4

32.♕b4! After playing a horrendous opening, Hikaru fights with only moves. To be honest, I was expecting him to hold this position at this point, but right on the next move he inexplicably stumbled.
32...♕c7

33.♗xe4?? This just loses by force. White was probably exhausted after having had to defend a terribly ugly position for so long. The most obvious move was 33.♔c1! which, had he seen that the capture on e4 is losing, Hikaru certainly would have made. Black is still better here, but his advantage is already far from decisive.

33...a5! A nice finesse, but apparently not the only way. 33...♕f4+ is simple, but also strong: 34.♔d3 ♘xe4! 35.♕xe4 ♖xc3+ 36.♗xc3 ♕xe4, and Black has way too many pawns not to win this position.
34.♕xb7 ♕f4+ 35.♔e2 ♖c7! 36.♕b6 ♘xe4 37.♕d4+ ♔h7 38.c4
38.♖gf1 was more stubborn, but after 38...♘xc3+ 39.♕xc3 ♕xf1+! the rook endgame is lost for White.

38...♖d7! And Black wins the queen.
39.♕e3 After 39.♕xd7, 39...♕f2+ 40.♔d3 ♘c5+ is a cute mechanism: 41.♔c3 ♘xd7. **39...♘g3+ 40.♕xg3 ♕xg3 41.♖xd7 ♕e5+** White resigned. A tense game!

To be honest, I was very disappointed to see the result of this game, as I was eager to be the decisive factor in the final GP standings. However, Hikaru, my opponent in the last round, was now half a point behind and since Gelfand had the white pieces against Ponomariov, Caruana was in another must-win situation with the black pieces, this time versus Dominguez.

My game went according to plan. With me never being in any danger as White and having a free push, Caruana could relax about this one. Gelfand-Ponomariov also seemed to be going quite according to the miracle scenario, as Ponomariov started the game with the fighting Dutch defence (let me remind you that back in my prime I once beat Boris with black in that exact same opening). As if on purpose, Dominguez played an interesting novelty in the topical Taimanov Variation... only to force a draw (although it was less forced than it may seem and perhaps Fabiano might have considered playing on somehow). Unfortunately, the intrigue died pretty fast, as Gelfand and Ponomariov started repeating moves very early on.

And so Shakhriyar Mamedyarov, watching from home, could finally breathe freely, knowing his schedule for March 2014. ∎

SECRETS OF OPENING SURPRISES

Magnus Carlsen and the  approach

Jeroen Bosch

As the chess world is eagerly looking forward to the upcoming match for the World Championship, it is tempting to speculate on all aspects of that battle. The final result is a prime source of speculation, of course, but so are the size and composition of the two teams, the influence of home ground versus foreign soil, and opening preparation or practical skills. Will the reigning World Champion once again manage to defend his title on the strength of his enormous experience? Anand played his first title match in 1995, when Magnus was four years old. Or will the Elo figures prove merciless and will youth and ambition prevail in the end?

One aspect always of interest in matches for the World Championship is the opening strategy of both giants, which often determine the fashion for years to come. Will we see a battle in respectable opening systems like the Ruy Lopez and the Queen's Gambit? Indeed, mastery of both has often been deemed essential for anyone aspiring to the highest crown. Will we see a principled struggle in which headstrong opponents lock horns over one line (the Berlin Wall and the 2000 Kasparov-Kramnik match spring to mind)? Or will one matador have a huge surprise in store for the other? Besides Kramnik's sudden adoption of the Berlin Wall we could mention Kasparov successfully springing the Dragon on an unsuspecting Anand in 1995.

I don't want to speculate too much about the concrete openings that we will see in Chennai, but I do want to write on a certain aspect of the challenger's approach to the opening stage: his willingness to experiment and to adopt surprising opening variations that are off the beaten track, and sometimes even downright dubious.

Let's start with some juvenilia. The following game was played when Magnus was 12 years old. White is Italy's strongest female player IM Elena Sedina.

VG 1.11 – C46
Elena Sedina
Magnus Carlsen
Saint Vincent 2003

1.e4 e5 2.♘f3 ♘c6 3.♘c3 ♘f6 4.g3

4...♘xe4!? Not everyone has the audacity to sacrifice a piece in the opening in such a way. Still, it is not as bad as it looks. The main protagonist of 4.g3, Igor Glek, even wrote an article on this line for the second volume of the SOS series.

One of the main lines versus the Glek Variation is 4...d5 5.exd5 ♘xd5 6.♗g2 ♘xc3 7.bxc3 ♗d6 8.0-0 0-0.

5.♘xe4 d5 6.♘c3 d4

7.♗g2!
A psychologically clever response from the more experienced player. Rightly fearing the energy of youth

and opening preparation, Sedina just returns the piece to transpose into a well-known main line in the Glek Variation. It is interesting to see that in 2013 this has been the choice of all the white players confronted with this piece sacrifice (which is still played by players above 2400). What happens if White tries to keep his material?

– 7.♘b1? e4 8.♘g1 is very passive, and apart from the obvious optical compensation, even Houdini is convinced after 8...d3.

– 7.♘b5 a6 8.♘a3 e4 9.♘h4!? is an attempt to refute 4...♘xe4, but it cannot convince. Certainly 9...g5 should now be investigated, but even Glek's main line 9...♗xa3 10.bxa3 0-0 11.♗b2 ♖e8 12.♗e2 ♗h3 13.♗g4 ♗xg4 14.♕xg4 ♘e5 15.♕h3 ♘f3+ 16.♔d1 is not too convincing after 16...♕d5! (an improvement over Glek's 16...♕f6). Black has long-term compensation.

– 7.♘e4 is interesting and was played by grandmaster Smirin. After 7...f5 8.♘eg5 (without the insertion of g2-g3, so when White plays 4.♘xe5?!, the knight could retreat to g3) 8...e4 9.♗c4 White returns the piece for an attack on f7:

9...exf3 10.♘xf3 (10.♗f7+ ♔d7 11. ♗e6+ ♔e8 is a draw by repetition; 10.♘f7 ♕e7+ 11.♔f1 ♘e5 12.♘xe5 ♕xe5 13.♕xf3 ♕e4 is more or less alright for Black) 10...♕e7+ 11.♔f1 ♗e6 12.d3 ♗xc4 13.dxc4 ♕d7 14.♔g2 0-0-0, with equal chances, Smirin-Macieja, Czech Republic 2004.
7...dxc3 8.bxc3 ♗d6 9.0-0 0-0
This is the main line mentioned above in the comments to move 4. Both

sides have lost a move. Sedina was proved right in going for this, when after **10.♖b1 ♖b8 11.d4 ♗g4 12. h3** the young Magnus made the mistake of playing

12...♗h5? when White won material after **13.g4 ♗g6 14.dxe5 ♘xe5** Stronger is 14...♗c5 15.♕e2 ♕d5 16. ♖b5!, as played in Glek-Berzinsh, Biel 1997, the game in which 12...♗h5? was played for the first time.
15.♘xe5 ♗xe5 16.♕xd8 ♖fxd8 17.f4!

After **17...♗xc2 18.♖b2 ♗d3 19. fxe5 ♗xf1 20.♗xf1** the bishops gave White an overwhelming endgame advantage.

I don't think that Carlsen's choice of opening was to blame here. Indeed, he was playing a decent IM with black, which means that there is no guarantee that anything else would have fared better. And after all, he ended up in what is a main line versus the Glek Variation, and one that is certainly OK for Black.

The previous year Magnus had already played the same piece sacrifice in a slightly different form.

SO 1.5 – C46
Magnus Carlsen
Sampsa Nyysti
Helsinki 2002

1.e4 e5 2.♘f3 ♘c6 3.♘c3 ♘f6 4. a3

In New In Chess 2001/8, I wrote on this move, naming it the Gunsberg Variation, after Isidor Gunsberg, a challenger of Wilhelm Steinitz for the World Championship. There are many lines in which the insipid-looking extra move a2-a3 is quite useful. One of Black's best lines is **4...g6** when I mentioned the piece sacrifice **5.♘xe5!? ♘xe5 6.d4 ♘c6**

7.d5 with the verdict that White has considerable compensation, while I added that 7.e5 ♘g8 8.♗c4 d6, as in R.Hendriks-Jonkman, Zwolle 2001, was insufficient. Possibly Magnus had read our favourite Magazine and was willing to try it out. With **7...♘b8** Nyysti showed that he was willing to pick up the gauntlet, but this is an even worse version, as the little pawn move a3 comes in handy. 7...♗g7 8. dxc6 bxc6 would have been Sedina's choice, as we know. Here, too, White

has the extra move a3, but this is now of little consequence.
8.e5 ♘g8 9.d6! cxd6 10.exd6 ♕f6
10...♗g7? loses to 11.♘d5.
11.♘b5 ♘a6 12.♗c4

White has very dangerous compensation.
12...♗h6 13.♕e2+?!
13.0-0.
13...♔f8 14.♗e3 ♗xe3 15.fxe3 ♕h4+ 16.g3 ♕h5 17.♕f2 ♕f5 18.♕e2
Or 18.♕xf5 gxf5 19.0-0 and even without queens White has compensation.
18...♕h5 19.♕f2 ♕f5 20.♕e2 ♘h6
Black spurns the repetition.
21.♖f1 ♕h5 22.♕f2 ♕f5 23.♕e2 ♕e5?! Here, too, Black should have repeated moves.
24.0-0-0

White has more than enough for the piece now. All his pieces have been deployed, whereas Black's queenside is undeveloped.
24...♔g7 25.♖d5 ♕e8 26.♕d2 ♖f8 27.♕d4+ f6 28.g4! b6
After 28...♘g8 29.g5 Black is also defenceless.

29.g5 ♘f5 30.gxf6+ ♖xf6 31. ♖dxf5! gxf5 32.♖g1+ and Magnus won.

In 2005, the small Dutch town of Schagen saw an interesting rapid round-robin between three talented Dutchmen and Magnus Carlsen (aged 14 and rated 2581) – incidentally won by Jan Smeets with 4½ out of 6, ahead of Carlsen, Stellwagen and l'Ami, all on minus 1. In one of the lunch breaks I had the pleasure of walking through a sunny Schagen with Magnus and his father. To my surprise the young grandmaster (and his father!) knew all about the SOS publications – although I should have guessed this perhaps, as Magnus was after all the first ever winner of the SOS Prize for his magnificent win over Sergey Dolmatov in 2004.

HD 13.6 – A04
Magnus Carlsen
Sergey Dolmatov
Moscow 2004

1.♘f3 f5 2.d3!?

The Improved Lisitsin Gambit, as I dubbed it in New In Chess 2002/3. 2.e4 fxe4 3.♘g5 is the original Lisitsin Gambit. The text looks passive, but is much more difficult to meet than 2.e4: White is preparing e4 under more favourable circumstances.
2...d6 How dangerous this line is, can be seen from 2...♘f6 3.e4! fxe4 4.dxe4, and now 4...♘xe4? (4...e5 is better, but White has an edge after 5.♗c4) is too risky: 5.♗d3 ♘f6 6.♘g5 g6 7.h4 (or 7.♘xh7 ♖xh7 8.♗xg6+ ♔f7 9.g4) 7...

d6 8.h5 (White is better) 8...gxh5? 9.
♗xh7 ♘xh7 10.♕xh5+ ♔d7 11.♘f7
♘g5, and Black resigned at the same
time in Lisitsin-Krogius, Leningrad
1949.

3.e4 e5 4.♘c3 ♘c6

4...c5 has been suggested by some to
avoid the dangers that face Black in
the game. 4...♘f6 5.exf5 ♗xf5 6.d4! e4
7.♘h4 also scores well for White.

5.exf5 ♗xf5 6.d4 ♘xd4

6...♘b4 7.♗b5+ c6 8.♗a4 e4 9.♘g5
d5 10.f3! exf3 11.0-0! was much better for White in Krasenkow-Kinder-
mann, Panormo 2001.

7.♘xd4 exd4 8.♕xd4

8...♘f6

Up until this game, the theory had
cited this position as satisfactory for
Black on the basis of a game Roman-
ishin-Malaniuk. Carlsen changed that
verdict rather convincingly.

8...c6 is not much better: 9.♗f4
♗xc2 10.♔d2! ♗g6 11.♖e1+ ♔d7
(11...♔f7? 12.♗c4+ d5 13.♘xd5!,
winning) 12.g3!? ♕b6 13.♗h3+!
♔d8 (13...♔c7 14.♗xd6+! ♗xd6
15.♕xg7+ ♔b8 16.♔c1! ♕xf2 17.
♘e4 was my analysis in SOS-2, with
the verdict that White is winning.
Surprisingly, the expert on the Dutch,
Vladimir Malaniuk, repeated all this
in a rapid game and duly lost: 17...
♗f4+ 18.gxf4 ♕xf4+ 19.♘d2 ♕f6
20.♕d7 ♕f8 21.♖e8+ 1-0, Fressi-
net-Malaniuk, Bastia rapid 2010) 14.
♗g5+ ♔c7 15.♘d5+ 1-0, Seel-Horst-
mann, Bad Wiessee 2003.
The immediate 8...♗xc2 is also met by
9.♗c4.

9.♗c4 A clear improvement over 9.

♗d3 ♗xd3 10.♕xd3 c6 11.0-0 ♗e7

12.♘e4 ♘xe4 13.♕xe4 0-0 14.c4 ♗f6
15.♗e3 d5 16.cxd5 ½-½, Roman-
ishin-Malaniuk, Tallinn 1987.

9...c6 10.♗g5 b5

White is also much better after the
more natural 10...d5 11.0-0-0 ♗e7
12.♕e5! ♗g6 13.♖he1.

11.♗b3 ♗e7 12.0-0-0 ♕d7 13. ♖he1 ♔d8?

After 13...0-0-0 both 14.♕f4 and 14.
g4 ♗xg4 15.♖xe7 are very powerful.

14.♖xe7! A winning sacrifice; the

whole game smacks of Morphy's play.

14...♕xe7

14...♔xe7 15.♗xf6+ gxf6 16.♖e1+
also wins.

15.♕f4! ♗d7 16.♘e4 d5

16...♖f8 17.♘xd6, winning.

17.♘xf6 h6 18.♗h4 g5 19.♕d4

and Dolmatov resigned, as 19...gxh4
20.♘xd5 is curtains.

A great game by Carlsen, and a successful example of his opening
approach. Simen Agdestein makes
an interesting observation in *Wonderboy* with which I would concur.

He emphasizes that although he usually advises his pupils to play the main
lines, it is in the case of Magnus (and
his huge talent) that alternating these
main lines with less orthodox variations becomes a good idea to push his
development even further.

We have seen some examples of a
young Magnus playing SOS lines. Let's
now leave Carlsen's juvenilia for what
they are, and take a look at his 'SOS
approach' in the last three years or so.
Let's start with what I would call an
extreme example.

KF 2.2 – B06
Michael Adams
Magnus Carlsen
Khanty-Mansiysk Olympiad
2010

1.e4 g6 2.d4 ♘f6 3.e5 ♘h5

Carlsen went on to lose the game, and
this result invoked a lot of criticism on
his opening choice. In an interview his
former coach Garry Kasparov considered it an insult to Adams to play in
such a way, and opined that Carlsen's
loss was deserved. Let's follow the game
for some more moves.

4.♗e2 A normal developing move

that attacks the knight, but if you play
like Adams then 4.♘f3 may well be
stronger. After 4...d6 White can then
continue with 5.♗c4.

4...d6

As advocated by Rolf Martens, who
dubbed the whole line the North Sea
Defence. The idea is that Black will
have considerable compensation after
5.♗xh5 gxh5 6.♕xh5.

Indeed, Black is fine after 6...dxe5 7. dxe5 ♕d5 when he will soon retrieve his pawn. And after 7.♕xe5 ♗g8 White has a pawn, but Black has some pressure and an important light-squared bishop.

In the game Adams avoided all this and continued sensibly (but not necessarily very ambitiously) with **5.♘f3 ♘c6 6.exd6 exd6**

Also playable is 6...♕xd6.

7.d5 ♘e7 8.c4 ♗g7 9.♘c3 0-0 10.0-0

It would be correct to state that Adams holds a slight plus here. However, Black surely has a playable position. Carlsen himself made a fair comment on the game on his weblog: 'Despite the unusual opening choice I was happy with my position entering the middlegame. Becoming a bit too optimistic I played for a win but underestimated his attack and lost deservedly.' Note that both Kasparov and Carlsen agree on the fact that Black deserved to lose this game, but while Kasparov condemned the *opening*, Carlsen condemned his subsequent *play*.

On the basis of this game I wrote an SOS article admitting that I had already stored away this idea in my file with SOS ideas for some time, but had considered it too dubious until Magnus came along and just played it. In my introduction to that article I invoked the spirit of the Dutch historian Johan Huizinga to call Magnus Carlsen a true 'Homo Ludens'. By a very curious incidence, the very next article in that same issue of New In Chess Magazine is one by Jonathan

> **'Both Kasparov and Carlsen agree on the fact that Black deserved to lose this game, but while Kasparov condemned the *opening*, Carlsen condemned his subsequent *play*.'**

Rowson entitled 'Homo Ludens'. I kid thee not! Rowson at some point in his argument emphasizes that chess is a game that we *play*.

This may seem rather obvious, but I think that this is a crucial point in understanding the choices that Carlsen makes when it comes to the opening. The Norwegian does not claim to be a scientist. He does not set out to prove that, say, the Ruy Lopez Breyer is the most correct choice against 1.e4, nor does he set his engines to work to analyse the Grünfeld to a forced draw. He just *plays* the game! This means that Carlsen has a different mindset from many other top players. All he needs from the opening is a playable position (with

slightly better, slightly worse or equal chances) and then he will just do that at which he is best: *playing* chess.

Let us see what other opening experiments Carlsen has allowed himself in recent years. I will exclude rapid and blitz games, because here most players allow themselves more leeway.

SO 5.8 – C45
Magnus Carlsen
Etienne Bacrot
Nanjing 2010

1.e4 e5 2.♘f3 ♘c6 3.d4 exd4 4.♘xd4 ♗c5 5.♘b3

By far the most popular move is 5.♗e3, and 5.♘xc6 is also played more often than the knight retreat.

5...♗b6 6.♘c3

Here 6.a4 is the classical main line, but Carlsen wants to castle queenside.

6...♘f6 7.♕e2!?

A great idea, and still fairly novel at the time (although Carlsen clearly isn't the inventor of this line). It leads to exciting positions with castling on opposite sides.

7...0-0 8.♗g5 h6 9.♗h4 a5 10.a4 ♘d4 11.♕d3 ♘xb3 12.cxb3 ♖e8 13.0-0-0 d6 14.♕c2

Black's next move is wrong, but as Landa observes in SOS-13, White has the slightly better chances anyway, while, interestingly, the engines find this hard to fathom (undoubtedly because of the doubled b-pawns). After **14...♗d7? 15.♗c4 ♗e6 16. ♖he1 ♕e7 17.e5 dxe5 18.♖xe5** Bacrot was under serious pressure and lost hopelessly.

VO 14.14 – D07
Vladimir Kramnik
Magnus Carlsen
London Chess Classic 2010

1.d4 d5 2.c4 ♘c6

Though not a sideline as such, the Chigorin Defence is not the most respectable of openings. Rather than enter any forced lines, Kramnik opts for a quiet, yet venomous continuation.

3.♘f3 ♗g4

4.♘c3

One month later Grischuk went for one of the principal lines in the Chigorin with 4.cxd5 ♗xf3 5.gxf3 ♕xd5 6.e3 e5 7.♘c3 ♗b4 8.♗d2 ♗xc3 9.bxc3

9...♘ge7 (this is not very popular – 9...♕d6, as played for example in Kasparov-Smyslov, Vilnius Candidates' match final (11) 1984, is the main line. Even in an offbeat opening Carlsen will be the first to leave the beaten track!) 10.c4 ♕d6 11.d5 ♘b8 12.♖b1 b6 13.♗b4 c5 14.dxc6 ♕xc6 (14...♕xd1+ 15.♖xd1 ♘bxc6 looks more logical, but, even though his structure is fractured, White is better due to his bishop pair) 15.♗d3 ♕e6 16.c5?! (strong looks 16.♖g1 g6 17. ♗e4 ♘bc6 18.♗d5) 16...♘bc6 17.cxb6

♘xb4 18.♖xb4 axb6 19.♕b3, and draw agreed – when the queens come off there is nothing left to play for – Grischuk-Carlsen, Wijk aan Zee 2011.

4...e6 5.♗f4 ♗d6 6.♗g3 ♘f6 7.e3 0-0 8.a3 ♘e7 9.♕b3

Kramnik aims to put pressure on the queenside. Carlsen uses his edge in development to more or less solve his problems.

9...b6 10.♘e5 c5 11.♘xg4 ♘xg4 12.♖d1 ♗xg3 13.hxg3 ♘f6 14. cxd5 exd5 15.♗e2 ♕d6 Now the position looks respectable again. Kramnik later outplayed Carlsen to obtain a winning position, only to squander it in the end. Carlsen managed to hang on by the skin of his teeth.

KP 4.10 – C41
Fabiano Caruana
Magnus Carlsen
Biel 2011

1.e4 d6 2.d4 ♘f6 3.♘c3 e5 4.♘f3 ♘bd7 5.♗c4 ♗e7 6.0-0 0-0 7.a4 a6!?

Philidor's Defence is in itself pretty respectable, but this is a sideline (7... c6 is normal).

8.a5 h6

9.♖e1

In 2013 Magnus repeated the whole line in the blitz tournament at the start of the Norway Supreme Masters (yes, I know I promised not to mention any blitz games!): 9.h3 ♖e8 10.♖e1 exd4 11.♘xd4 ♘e5 12.♗f1 c5 13.♘f5 ♗f8 14.♘e3 ♗e6 15.♘ed5 ♘c6 16.♘xf6+ ♕xf6 17.♘d5 ♗xd5 18.♕xd5 ♖e5 19.♕b3 ♖b8?! (19...♘d4 20.♕xb7 ♖ae8) 20.c3?! (20.♗c4!) 20...d5! 21. ♖d1 c4 22.♕c2 dxe4 23.♗e3 ♘xa5! 24.♗d4 ♘b3 25.♗xe5 ♕xe5, and with two pawns for the exchange Black was better, although he later lost (it was a blitz game, after all), Karjakin-Carlsen, Stavanger 2013.

9...exd4 10.♘xd4

Black immediately equalizes after 10.♕xd4 ♘e5! 11.♘xe5 dxe5 12.♕xd8 (12.♕xe5?? ♗d6 traps the queen!) 12...♖xd8, Smeets-Movsesian, Wijk aan Zee 2013.

10...♘e5 11.♗f1 c5

Here 11...♖e8 12.b3 c5 13.♘f5 ♗xf5 14.exf5 ♘c6 15.♗b2 d5 favoured Black in Pelletier-Hauchard, Biel 2010.

12.♘b3 ♗e6 13.♗f4 ♖c8 14.h3 ♖e8 15.♗xe5 dxe5 16.♘d2 c4

And Black had an easy game.

EO 24.10 – A20
Vladimir Kramnik
Magnus Carlsen
Moscow Tal Memorial 2011

1.c4 e5 2.g3 ♘f6 3.♗g2 h6!?

It looks odd, but this move is generally useful in the English Opening, and this is an idea of the famous Moldavian trainer Viacheslav Chebanenko. Igor Glek wrote on this line for SOS-5.

4.♘c3 ♗b4 5.e4 ♘c6

Glek himself played 5...♗xc3 6.bxc3 0-0 7.♘e2 ♖e8 8.0-0 c6, Cekro-Glek, Vlaardingen rapid, 2005.

6.♘ge2 ♗c5 7.d3

7.0-0 a6 8.a3 d6 9.b4 ♗a7 10.h3 ♘d4 was OK for Black in Cekro-Jaracz, Belgium 2003/04.

7...d6 8.h3 ♘h7

This won't solve Black's problems, but other moves won't either, according to Timman, who analysed the game in New In Chess 2011/8. The Dutch grandmaster asks an interesting question with reference to Carlsen's opening play in this particular game: 'What would happen if you gave away several tempos in the opening: would this mean that your opponent would already be winning?'.

9.a3 a6 10.0-0 ♘g5 11.♔h2 ♘e6 12.f4 ♗d7 13.b4 ♗a7 14.♘d5 ♘ed4 15.♘ec3 ♗e6 16.f5 ♗d7 17.♖b1 ♘b8 18.c5 dxc5 19.bxc5 ♗c8

It is obvious that White is superior, but after wild complications the game ended in a draw. I refer you to Timman's analysis of this fantastic fight.

SI 2.2 – B53
Magnus Carlsen
Gawain Jones
London Chess Classic 2012

1.e4 c5 2.♘f3 d6 3.d4

Carlsen rarely enters the terrain of the Open Sicilian (will he allow Anand to play the Najdorf in Chennai?).

'I don't think it is very realistic to think that I can beat Anand in the opening. That's not where my strength is.'

In 2013 he only did so versus Nakamura (a win in a Kalashnikov side-line with 6.g3), and Ivanchuk (a loss in a Taimanov). Here he opts for the Hungarian Variation, which is closer in spirit to the 3.♗b5(+) Sicilians that Carlsen often plays. In 2013 Carlsen adopted an interesting and fairly new SOS-like line against Peter Svidler in the Norway Supreme Masters: 3. ♗b5+ ♘d7 4.0-0 a6 5.♗d3!?.

3...cxd4 4.♕xd4 a6 5.h3!?

This had earlier been played by Areschenko and Ni Hua, but at the time there were only a few games with 5.h3.

5...♘c6 6.♕e3 g6 7.c4 ♗g7 8.♗e2 ♘f6 9.♘c3 0-0 10.0-0 ♘d7 11.♖b1 a5 12.b3 ♘c5 13.♗b2

Both sides are OK, but Carlsen was presumably happy to just play the position. White won.

KP 8.7 – C44
Magnus Carlsen
Pentala Harikrishna
Wijk aan Zee 2013

1.e4 e5 2.♘f3 ♘c6 3.c3!?

The Ponziani Opening is a very rare guest on the highest level.

3...♘f6 The other main line versus the Ponziani is 3...d5 4.♕a4 and now 4...♘f6?! 5.♘xe5 ♗d6 6.♘xc6 bxc6 7. d3 0-0 8.♗e2 ♖e8 9.♘d2 ♗f4 10.0-0 ♗xd2 11.♗xd2 dxe4 12.d4 with an edge, Ghaem Maghami-Harikrishna, Ha Long City (rapid) 2009.

4.d4 d5!? Carlsen himself opted for 4...exd4 5.e5 ♘d5 when confronted by the Ponziani at the hands of a cheeky Hou Yifan. (Hou Yifan-Carlsen, Wijk aan Zee 2013).

The main line is 4...♘xe4 5.d5 and now 5...♘e7 or 5...♘b8.

5.♗b5! exd4 6.e5 ♘e4 7.♘xd4 ♗d7 8.♗xc6 bxc6 9.0-0
White has an extra tempo compared to the Two Knights Defence (3.♗c4 ♘f6 4.d4 exd4 5.e5 d5 6.♗b5 ♘e4 7.♘xd4) – Carlsen has gained the additional tempo c2-c3. As Carlsen commented after the game: 'With an extra move it must be something'.
9...♗e7 10.♗e3 0-0 11.♘d2 ♘c5 12.b4! ♘b7 13.f4 a5! 14.f5! axb4 15.cxb4 ♗xb4 16.♕g4!

And White had a very dangerous initiative for the pawn. Carlsen went on to win a nice game.

QP 7.9 – A45
Magnus Carlsen
Vladimir Kramnik
Moscow Tal Memorial 2013

Magnus often singles out Vladimir Kramnik for his opening experiments. Or, as the Norwegian observed himself tongue in cheek in New In Chess 2013/5, when playing Kramnik, 'My main concern has been how to equalize, even with white.'

1.d4 ♘f6 2.♗g5 d5 3.e3 c5

'The best way to handle the Trompowsky,' according to Carlsen in his analysis. **4.♗xf6 gxf6 5.dxc5** Here I would prefer 5.♘c3, which transposes to the Richter-Veresov. **5...e6 6.♘f3 ♘d7 7.c4 dxc4 8.c6 ♘b6 9.♘bd2 c3 10.bxc3 bxc6 11.♕c2 ♗g7 12.♗d3 f5 13.e4 ♕f6**

And Black had a very decent game, but Magnus kept grinding away and won on move 72.

In his final test before the World Championship match, the Sinque-field Cup in St. Louis, Carlsen adopted the Leningrad Dutch versus Aronian (and obtained a good position). However, some might say that the Dutch is a respectable opening, although I am afraid that we have to go back to the times of Botvinnik to see it in a match for the World Championship.

I hope that I have convinced you that Carlsen's approach to the opening is highly idiosyncratic. The challenger is not aiming for an opening advantage (or equality) in the traditional sense. His intention is to *play*. And in order to reach playable positions, almost anything goes. Thus, he will play the main lines when he feels like it, but he is equally willing to leave the beaten track when the situation (or his mood) requires it. If needs be he won't even avoid dubious lines (his game against Adams at the 2010 Olympiad), and will experiment almost for experiment's sake. Fun is another important aspect of the game that is played by the sportsman and *Homo Ludens* Magnus Carlsen.

In a recent interview with Chess TV, the Russian internet TV channel, Carlsen candidly talked about his opening strategy (it was just after the 2013 Tal Memorial), and I should like to end this article by quoting Carlsen:
'[My] approach was to play something unexpected that I haven't really played before, not necessarily to get a big advantage but to get some playable positions. ... I think that Anand and others are so strong in the opening that it might not make sense for me with my skillset to try and beat him in the opening. I will certainly prepare some surprises and try to outfox him in a way, but I don't think it is very realistic that I can try to beat him in the opening. That's not where my strength is.' ∎

Jeroen Bosch is the editor of the SOS series (Secrets of Opening Surprises) published by New In Chess. Last August FIDE's Trainers' Commission awarded him the Isaac Boleslavsky medal for his work as a chess author.

Doctors, psychiatrists and extreme dentistry

For his match against Anand, Magnus Carlsen resurrected a clause that allows postponement of a game in case of illness. After reading about the early history of World Championship matches, Hans Ree got the impression that champions and challengers might have dropped dead at the board without such a clause.

In his story 'The House of Asterion', Jorge Luis Borges retells the Greek myth about the Minotaur – the monster with the body of a man and the head of a bull – but not from the usual perspective of Theseus, who slayed the monster, but from that of the Minotaur himself.

In his infinite labyrinth, Asterion – the name of the Minotaur – is lonely. He plays sad games, for example running through the stone galleries until he drops dizzily on the floor, or letting himself fall from a roof until he is bloody. His favourite game is pretending that there is another Asterion who occasionally comes to visit him to be shown the house, the labyrinth that is as large as the world. Sometimes they laugh heartily together.

Every nine years, nine men (the myth says seven years and seven men, but Borges must have had a reason to make it nine) enter his house to be killed by him, and one of these men prophesied, at the moment of his death, that some day the Minotaur's redeemer would come.

Asterion reflects: 'Since then my loneliness does not pain me, because I know my redeemer lives and he will finally rise above the dust. If my ear could capture all the sounds of the world, I should hear his steps. I hope he will take me to a place with fewer galleries and fewer doors. What will my redeemer be like?, I ask myself. Will he be a bull or a man? Will he perhaps be a bull with the face of a man? Or will he be like me?' (translation James E. Irby)

The final words in Borges's story are those that Theseus says to Ariadne, the girl who had given him the ball of thread to find his way into the labyrinth. 'Would you believe it, Ariadne?' said Theseus. 'The Minotaur scarcely defended itself.'

To the reader, at least to me, only these last lines make clear what the story is about.

The lonely champion

I had read this story about 50 years ago and when I was pondering about this article about world championship matches, it came back to my mind. No wonder. The lonely Minotaur, fantasizing about his double, with whom he has a laugh, and about the redeemer who will slay him – these two are the same persons in different guise – strongly suggests, to a chess player at least, an older World Champion who has beaten everyone and is now waiting at home to be relieved of his burden by a Theseus of chess.

Maybe the theme is running away with me; we shouldn't push the analogy too far.

Like most people, I consider Magnus Carlsen to be the favourite in his match against Anand, but I do not at all expect it to be as one-sided as the clash between Theseus and the Minotaur. It would be silly to predict the outcome of a tough chess match between two great players on the basis of a Greek myth.

Borges has written a poem with the title *Ajedrez* (Chess), and he often alluded to chess in his stories. In an interview he said that chess was one of the means we have to save the culture, like Latin, reading the classics, studying the humanities... He also mentioned some other endangered niches of learning.

I wondered if Borges himself had considered the similarity between the Minotaur in his den and a World Chess Champion, or whether it was just a fantasy of my own. Jan Timman, who like me is a great admirer of Borges, had the privilege of meeting him for a long conversation in Buenos Aires in 1982, so he may have asked him this question, but I don't know whether he did. There were many other things to talk about.

Theseus brings his cook

To me it seems only right that the challenger visits the champion in his own territory, but it hasn't often happened in chess history. In 1894 Emanuel Lasker came to Wilhelm (or maybe William by that time) Steinitz's U.S, and in 1937 Alekhine came to Euwe's Netherlands, though you may wonder if Alekhine really considered himself to be the challenger. Russian writers in particular have made it appear as if Alekhine came to the Netherlands in 1937 to collect a title that he had given on loan to Euwe two years earlier. I don't agree with this point of view.

When Johannes Zukertort came to the U.S. in 1886 for the first official world championship match, he wasn't the challenger and Steinitz wasn't the champion, though in retrospect it may well appear so. Officially they were on an equal footing.

And now Magnus Carlsen does it the right way – visiting the champion on his home turf, although for several reasons he did it only reluctantly. What about the climate, and what about the change of diet, with dangerous foreign germs waiting for him? As we could read in the previous issue of New In Chess, Carlsen, when he went to Chennai on an inspection tour last August, was accompanied by his cook, who will prepare his food during the match.

And to be on the safe side, Carlsen has resurrected an old rule that was abolished quite some time ago: postponement of a game in case of illness. How many times a player may ask for a postponement I don't know. On the FIDE website it still says that no game can be postponed at all.

Some Indian media didn't like Carlsen's illness clause and suggested that it was a novelty in chess history, but their memory is short. A similar clause was in effect in 1886 and since then it was standard practice for about a century.

Magnus Carlsen received a warm welcome when in August he arrived in Chennai for a brief inspection tour. It was the first time the world's number one visited India.

Insomnia and worse

Bad health, especially that of Zukertort, played quite a big role in that match of 1886. Steinitz was 49 years old. Zukertort was 43, but in a frail condition.

Years of acrimonious negotiations had preceded the match.

'Experience has taught me that every direct contact with Mr. Steinitz exhausts all human patience and proves to be fruitless,' wrote Zukertort in 1885 in the English magazine *Chess Monthly*. Steinitz reacted in his *International Chess Magazine* by making fun of Zukertort's supposed doctor's title and threatening that his second would protest against Zukertort's illegitimate use of it.

Making a jump in history, I think that some of Alekhine's colleagues knew that he had no right to call himself Dr. Alekhine, but as far as I know they kept this knowledge to themselves. And why not? The learned company of Dr. Lasker, Dr. Tarrasch, Dr. Tartakower, Dr. Euwe and Dr. Vidmar might well have considered it an honour that Alekhine was so keen on joining them.

Zukertort departed from Liverpool on December 5th, 1885, and arrived in New York on December 13th. The first match game was played in New York on January 11th, 1886, and the last one in New Orleans on March 29th. In between they had played in St. Louis, nowadays the centre of American chess.

Almost three months of chess is quite a long time for modern standards, but the match could have lasted longer if Zukertort had put up stronger resistance. The match was for 10 wins and took only 20 games with the result +10 −5 =5 in favour of Steinitz.

Steinitz complained about nervousness and insomnia, which you might call the normal professional hazards, but Zukertort was in a much worse state. Before the match he had already been warned by his doctor that serious chess would be dangerous to his fragile health. Nevertheless, in New York, after losing the first game, Zukertort won four games in a row. But already then, while leading 4-1, he appears to have confided to the American master Max Judd that he would lose the match. And indeed, of the last 15 games he would win only one.

A wreck in body and spirit

Near the end, observers described Zukertort as a wreck in body and spirit. He couldn't concentrate anymore and spent far too little time on his moves. In the last game Steinitz played his eccentric Steinitz gambit, 1.e4 e5 2.♘c3 ♘c6 3.f4 exf4 4.d4. Zukertort had to resign after only 18 moves.

Two years later, Zukertort suffered a stroke while playing chess at Simpson's Divan in London and died the next day, only 45 years old. Having been warned to give up chess once again, he had said, according to the *Oxford Companion to Chess*, 'I am prepared to be taken away at any moment.'

Tarrasch, a physician by profession, later wrote that the match against Steinitz had cost Zukertort his life. Domański and Lissowski, Zukertort's biographers, do not so much blame this particular match as the unhealthy lifestyle of the bohemian chess professional in general.

For the match, Zukertort had received 750 dollars to cover his expenses, but no prize money. Steinitz had won, apart from 500 dollars for expenses, the stakes of 4,000 dollars, from which he had to give 3,000 dol-

lars to his backers. Even if you multiply these amounts by 20 – a rough estimate, as converting old money to its present value is tricky – it seems a very moderate reward.

Contradictory perspectives

For the match in which Steinitz would lose his crown to Lasker, in 1894, the conditions were practically the same as when he played Zukertort. Again both players (or rather their backers) submitted a stake of 2,000 dollars, again the match was for 10 wins and would be played in three North-American cities, this time New York, Philadelphia and Montreal.

I remember once reading an old newspaper report (don't know where, don't know when...) about a Dutch stand-up comedian in Amsterdam who commented on the latest result from Montreal, which suggests that there was quite a lot of world-wide interest in that match.

Again bad health played a role. Steinitz complained about arthritis and insomnia, and according to a *New York Times* report after the eighth game, Lasker was not in great condition either. Both players took up the three days' rest that were allowed them in case of illness.

Lasker won with the score +10 –4 =5, even slightly better than what Steinitz had achieved against Zukertort. Steinitz had turned 58 during the match, Lasker was 27.

Later, Tarrasch, who had already more or less implied that Steinitz had won the championship against only a shadow of Zukertort, wrote that his own victory in 1905 over the young Marshall certainly had more merit than Lasker's victory against the old Steinitz. He might have been silenced, although he wasn't, when, in 1907, Lasker beat Marshall with an even more overwhelming score than Tarrasch had done.

But it was true, Steinitz had been old and frail in 1894.

Jacques Hannak wrote in his book *Der Michelangelo des Schachspiels*: 'Therefore we fully tend to share the opinion of those who say that Lasker did not beat the chess player Steinitz, but the sick body of Steinitz.'

That's what many thought at the time, but for a different opinion I can refer you to the same Jacques Hannak, this time not in his hagiography about Steinitz, but in his book *Emanuel Lasker, Biographie eines Schachweltmeisters*:

'It was Steinitz's misfortune that he too didn't understand the spiritual superiority of Lasker, so much based on their characters, and that he didn't abdicate with a grand gesture, but threw himself, with a fanatical ferocity and confidence that would eventually lead to tragedy and catastrophe, ever again into battle, firmly convinced that he could still dethrone Lasker and that he had only failed against the younger man by the unfavourable physical circumstances.'

Here you see two completely different perspectives, though from the same writer, who in his Steinitz book had it that Lasker defeated only Steinitz's sick body, and in his Lasker book that Steinitz suffered from the tragical illusion that he had only lost because of bad health and not because of Lasker's spiritual superiority.

On the pages of New In Chess I have written some rather harsh things about Jacques Hannak, who all in all was quite an interesting writer. This is because as a youngster I was more taken by his florid pontifications than I am now.

In the doctor's hall

It may be called fitting that the revenge match between Lasker and Steinitz began on October 25th, 1896 (the Julian calendar, still in use then in Russia) at the Doctor's Assembly Hall in Moscow. The match had been postponed, though only for a few days, because Lasker had been ill.

After six games, with a score of +5

–0 =1 in favour of Lasker, the match was interrupted for 10 days because of Steinitz getting ill. When it was resumed, witnesses said that Steinitz often played while holding an icepack to his head. This rings true, as Steinitz was an ardent follower of the theories of the Bavarian priest Sebastian Kneipp in which ice-cold water was very important.

Then it was Lasker's turn to postpone a game due to illness. Later, in the second half of the 20th century, these postponements due to illness could be taken more or less at will, even by players who were actually in splendid health, but I think that at that time honour would forbid Steinitz and Lasker to claim illness without good reason.

Another postponement occurred on December 23rd, when both players appeared at the hall for their 17th and last game. They waited a half hour for the officials, who didn't appear, and then decided to postpone the game until December 30th. In the meantime, Lasker played a short match with a certain Boyarkov from the local chess circles.

Agony for a follower of Kneipp

In this revenge match, Lasker beat Steinitz with 10 wins, two losses and five draws. While it was in progress, Steinitz had written a letter to the *New York Sun* in which he stuck to his well-known dictum that a chess master has as little right to be sick as a general on the battlefield, but then, while giving Lasker his due as the best player he had ever met, possibly the best that had ever lived, he cited his ailments: insomnia and nervous exhaustion, which was aggravated by the Russians' fear of fresh air and their habit of overheating the rooms to an insufferable temperature – all anathema to a follower of Kneipp.

One day, Steinitz wrote, he had a fainting fit which might have been his end if a friend had not saved him in time.

And there was more to come. Still in Moscow, Steinitz had a nervous breakdown and on February 11th, 1897 (I think Steinitz's biographer Kurt Landsberger, to whom I owe most of these details, is using the Gregorian calendar now), he was committed to the Morosov Clinical Hospital for the Insane. One of his doctors was the famous neuropsychiatrist Sergey Korsakov.

Soon afterwards it was reported that Steinitz had died, which made Tarrasch write an obituary for the *Deutsche Schachzeitung* (never published) which he was to show a year later to Steinitz, who according to Tarrasch was quite pleased with it.

The Jews know how to advertise themselves

Near the end of his life Steinitz would write that he had been quite amused when he found out that an anti-Semitic Austrian paper had written, after it had learned that the report about his death was not true: The Jews know how to advertise themselves.

During his hospitalization Steinitz wrote a letter to a friend, which contained the famous and very reasonable quip that 'like all fools I am imagining that all doctors are crazier than me.'

Landsberger quotes many accounts of the nature of Steinitz's condition, without being able to reach a firm conclusion.

Steinitz was released on March 12th, and four days later left Moscow for Vienna to find some chess there.

During his final years he still played a few important tournaments, with varying success. Back in New York, in 1900, he had another mental breakdown and was nursed for many months in several mental hospitals, supported by a fund that the Manhattan Chess Club had raised in view of his dire financial situation. He died on August 12th, 1900 in the Manhattan State Hospital, at the age of 64.

Again, just as in the case of Zukertort, it is impossible to say whether Steinitz's two last matches, with the pain and sorrow they involved, really contributed to his early death. It's at least plausible.

Some money, at last

The sad tale of bad health can be continued. Lasker easily defended his title in several matches, until after 27 years as World Champion he was beaten by José Raúl Capablanca.

For those who have been critical of FIDE in the past, with very good reason I must say, their match can be a reminder that international chess life without FIDE wasn't all wine and roses either.

Capablanca had already challenged Lasker in 1911. Three years of negotiations were interrupted by World War I. And after the war it took another three years until the match finally took place in Havana.

A year before the match, Lasker had taken the position that he preferred to hand over his title to Capablanca without playing, but as both Capablanca and the general chess world would not accept this, he went reluctantly to Capablanca's Cuba.

At least the financial conditions were better than before: a purse of 20,000 dollars, 11,000 of which would go to Lasker and 9,000 to Capablanca, whatever the result. During the match the

Commission for the Encouragement of Touring throughout Cuba donated an extra prize of 5,000 dollars, 3,000 of which were to go to the winner.

My best guess is that you should multiply these numbers by 13 to get their present value.

This time the match was for eight wins. Lasker resigned the match on the ground of bad health when the score was four wins for Capablanca, none for Lasker, and 10 draws. That this was no easy excuse is evident from the fact that Lasker, after his return to Europe, had to be hospitalized for several months.

And not for the first time either. In 1894, after his match against Steinitz, he had to be nursed in Germany by his physician brother Berthold for a long time, because his life was apparently in danger. In this case there were so many months between the match and his breakdown that it seems far-fetched to blame the curse of the world championship match.

Ordeal at the dentist

It was about time for a match between two healthy men at the height of their powers. Maybe the world championship match between Capablanca and Alekhine in 1927 can be described as such, although after losing that match Capablanca declared that he had been

in decline since 1917, and that anyway chess was not interesting enough to be fully committed to it.

Here is a quote from William Hartston's book *The Kings of Chess*: 'With wins in the eleventh and twelfth games, Alekhine stormed back into the lead. He even had a ready excuse for his poor play in the previous part of the match – he had had to have six teeth removed between games.'

Six teeth? The horror! I have once seen this done to one of my cats and I still cry. How could Alekhine go on beating Capablanca after this ordeal? I remember having read a things-to-do list in a notebook by Mikhail Botvinnik, as preparation for a championship match. One of these things to do before the match was a visit to the dentist. Real professionalism started with Botvinnik.

Botvinnik has said that a world championship match, with everything that it involves, would take one year off one's life. The early history of these matches suggests that they took off more than that. ∎

Hans Ree's new book My Chess *(240 pages, with a foreword by Jan Timman) has just been published by Russell Enterprises and is available from our webshop.*

Beware: Brilliancy! Solutions of page 83

1. Aronian-Carlsen
Moscow 2011

2. Anand-Sokolov
Wijk aan Zee 1996

3. Leko-Carlsen
Monaco rapid 2007

35...♖fg5! would have decided the game in Black's favour. The bishop ending following 36.♕xg5 ♖xg5 37.♔xg5 c5 38.♗c2 ♗e2 leaves White no hope.

The highly surprising 28.♖xa6!! ♕xa6 29.♘c5 ♕c6! (or 29...♖xf7 30.♖xf7+ ♔xf7 31.♘xe5+!) 30.♘e6+ ♕xe6 31. ♗xe6 ♖xf2 32.♔xf2 b3! 33.c3! ♖xd3 34.♔e2 ♖d8 35.♘d2! would have secured his advantage.

Black missed the invisible retreat 14...♕d8!!, after which he is winning in all variations, with the incredible highlight: 15.♔e2 ♗g4+ 16.♔f2 and now the study-like switch-back: 16...♕h4+!.

4. Anand-Bologan
Wijk aan Zee 2004

5. Svidler-Carlsen
London Candidates 2013

6. Anand-Kulaots
Tallinn Keres Memorial (rapid) 2004

White probably declined the other candidate move 18.b4! in view of 18...dxc3 (18...♗d6 19.bxa5 ♗xe5 20. ♗h7+ ♔h8 21.♖xe5, and White wins) 19.bxa5 ♕d4+ 20.♔h1 ♕xe5, overlooking the follow-up 21.♗a3!! ♖f1+ 22.♖xf1 ♗xa3 23.♖f5 ♕e8 24.♖e1 ♗f7 25.♕xc3 and wins.

The alternative was a direct attack against the enemy king: 25...♗xh3! 26.dxe4 (26.gxh3 ♕xh3 27.♗e3 ♖h5, winning) 26...♖g5 27.g3 ♗g4 28.f3 ♖b2! 29.♕xb2 ♗xf3 30.♖f1 30...♖xg3+ 31.♔f2 ♖g2+, winning the queen.

The forceful 27.♗d8!! would have shortened the struggle significantly: 27...♖axd8 28.♕xd8 ♖xd8 29.♖xd8+ ♗f8 30.♖ee8 h5 31.g6!! ♕g1+ 32.♔a2 ♕c5 33.♖xf8+ ♕xf8 34.♖xf8+ ♔xf8 35.b4 fxg6 36.b5, winning.

Peter Heine Nielsen

CURRENT ELO: **2649**

DATE OF BIRTH: **May 24, 1973**

PLACE OF BIRTH: **Holstebro, Denmark**

PLACE OF RESIDENCE: **Palanga, Lithuania**

What food makes you happy?
Vegetarian Indian and Thai. Japanese Sukiyaki. Quantity matters.

And what drink?
Freshly squeezed apple-juice.

Who is your favourite author?
Generally, I like Swedish authors Jan Guillou, Henning Mankell, Stieg Larsson, for the way they mix politics, women's rights and crime stories.

What was the most interesting book you ever read?
I read a lot about Game Theory, and it had a huge influence on me.

What is your all-time favourite movie?
Moneyball. Not just a great movie, it is also thought-provoking for a sports coach who values statistics.

What is your favourite TV series?
Yes Minister, Sherlock, Seinfeld I know by heart, but the list could be much longer.

What music do you like to listen to?
R.E.M., Green Day, Coldplay, even Metallica. In my youth I was a fan of Pink Floyd, while the best live performance I've seen was by the Rolling Stones.

What do you see as your best result ever?
Being part of team Vishy. My best results as a player were top-scorer in Amsterdam 2009 as well as getting to Round 4 in the 2011 World Cup.

What was the best game you ever played?
Against Kiril Georgiev in the 2000 Istanbul Olympiad.

Who is your favourite chess player of all time?
Kramnik's games, and especially his approach to openings, inspired me a lot both as a player and as a second. Ironically, I always seem to help his opponents, whether it is Fritz, Vishy or Magnus.

Is there a chess book that had a profound influence on you?
I read all of Larsen's books. His influence on my generation of Danish players cannot be overestimated.

What was the most exciting chess game you ever saw?
Game 12 from the Topalov-Anand match in Sofia.

What is the best chess country in the world?
Japan. In their version of chess (shogi) they have 150 federation-employed professionals, seven annual title-matches, television coverage etc.

What are chess players particularly good at (except for chess)?
Alternating periods of intense intellectual effort with complete relaxation (or should I say laziness?).

What is it that you appreciate most in a person?
Loyalty, emotional intelligence.

What is it that you dislike in a person?
Superficiality and showing off. I find it hard to believe you can squeeze a relevant point of view into 140 characters.

Who or what would you like to be if you weren't yourself?
A game theorist or a judge. Both are very interesting academically, as well as essential in a society.

Which three people would you like to invite for dinner?
Bill and Melinda Gates, and Warren Buffett. I'm really impressed with their philanthropic organization and the philosophy behind it.

What is the best piece of advice you were ever given?
Within one week my chess federation president told me to focus on my university studies, while my university teacher said I should definitely focus on chess.

Is there something you'd love to learn?
Baseball, shogi and golf are my biggest hobbies at the moment. And there is definitely a lot to learn.

What is the stupidest rule in chess?
It's a choice between zero-tolerance and dress-code. They do nothing to tackle actual problems.

What will be the nationality of the 2050 chess world champion?
I believe in numbers. China, Russia or India.

What is the best thing that was ever said about chess?
I once told Larsen it was good to put weaker players under pressure. He replied that it's always good to put *any* opponent under pressure. Apart from realizing that I'm a tad too cautious, I understood it's the best possible advice.